T0367296

Words of Praise for
Through Kenny's Eyes

In *Through Kenny's Eyes*, Ken and Carol Jones have written an extraordinary book about the liberation of experiencing death, dying, and grief from a spiritual perspective. Having known them both well, before Kenny's illness and at the time of his transition, we recognize and acknowledge the depth of their authentic self-expression about their journey through this challenging time. Their writing is genuine, insightful, and highly personal, and this book demonstrates an intimate sharing of the process of approaching one's own death and the death of a loved one with courage, humility, and profound acceptance. Carol shares her unique perspective of grief as well as the transformational experience available to anyone who is ready to embrace the dying of a loved one as an act of sacred service. This is a book that will touch many hearts and speaks to the spiritual opportunity of seeing transition through the eyes of a Spiritual Warrior.

—Drs. Ron and Mary Hulnick, co-directors of the
University of Santa Monica and authors of *Loyalty to
Your Soul: The Heart of Spiritual Psychology*

If you have any considerations or fears about dying, read this book and share it with others. It will shed light on your awareness about the mystery of death and help you relax about it. This book is a gift that must be opened.

—Agapi Stassinopoulos,
author of *Unbinding the Heart*

This book is an amazing gift for anyone to gain comfort and inspiration, guidance and courage. All of us will pass, and to know what the passages are in such humanity and ordinariness is the treasure of this account. The dance between Carol and Ken and the Mystical Traveler Consciousness is a teaching in itself. From the human to the transcendent. I will reference this book for my own experience and guidance. God's glory shines in it. Recommended reading for any course on death and dying.

—Leigh Taylor Young, Emmy award-winning actress, lover of
Spirit, life, and serving the good

Ken and Carol Jones share the stories of their journey from cancer diagnosis to passing from this world with the voice of Spirit guiding them. This book is a must for anyone who seeks greater understanding and acceptance of death and dying with a spiritual focus.

—Joe Hubbard, chief executive officer, Insight Seminars, partner and executive consultant for McGhee Productivity

As a hospice chaplain, I have shared dialogue about ongoing life after physical death, which I often experienced as do many of my patients' families after the deaths of their loved ones. Carol and Kenny embraced that reality before Kenny's death. Their story carries them forward, past what might otherwise have been relegated to an ending, but instead was a transition to Spirit, as I believe physical death is. Love never dies, and Carol and Kenny's story is one that will help those of different spiritual backgrounds who are grieving know the richness of the Spirit that survives the death of the body. What is important is not lost but deepens and remains essential.

—Pat Holden, hospice chaplain

Through Kenny's Eyes takes us beyond our cultural myth that dying is filled with pain and suffering and to be feared. It blesses us all with an awakening to the reality that the dying process is so filled with blessings and sacred energy, and in the end is a mystery. No two deaths are the same, and consciousness survives. As a hospice registered nurse for over three decades, I am deeply moved by this powerful account of the truth of the reality of death and dying.

—Denys Cope RN BSN, MSS, author of *Dying: a Natural Passage*

Through Kenny's Eyes

A Magnificent Journey from Illness to Ecstasy

The Frisky, the Jones family sneakbox sailboat moored
in Barnegat Bay at our beloved Island House
Photo by Ken Jones

CAROL AND KEN JONES

BALBOA.
PRESS
A DIVISION OF HAY HOUSE

Copyright © 2014 Carol and Ken Jones.

All rights reserved. No part of this book may be used or reproduced by
any means, graphic, electronic, or mechanical, including photocopying,
recording, taping or by any information storage retrieval system
without the written permission of the author except in the case of
brief quotations embodied in critical articles and reviews.

Balboa Press books may be ordered through booksellers or by contacting:

Balboa Press
A Division of Hay House
1663 Liberty Drive
Bloomington, IN 47403
www.balboapress.com
1 (877) 407-4847

Because of the dynamic nature of the Internet, any web addresses or
links contained in this book may have changed since publication and
may no longer be valid. The views expressed in this work are solely those
of the author and do not necessarily reflect the views of the publisher,
and the publisher hereby disclaims any responsibility for them.

The author of this book does not dispense medical advice or prescribe the use
of any technique as a form of treatment for physical, emotional, or medical
problems without the advice of a physician, either directly or indirectly. The
intent of the author is only to offer information of a general nature to help
you in your quest for emotional and spiritual well-being. In the event you use
any of the information in this book for yourself, which is your constitutional
right, the author and the publisher assume no responsibility for your actions.

Print information available on the last page.

ISBN: 978-1-4525-2275-3 (sc)
ISBN: 978-1-4525-2277-7 (hc)
ISBN: 978-1-4525-2276-0 (e)

Library of Congress Control Number: 2014917269

Balboa Press rev. date: 11/18/2015

For my darling Kenny, whose final ministry in this
life blossomed into the telling of our compelling
and unusual story through this book,
and for beloved John-Roger, our spiritual teacher and
"way shower," who made the universal teachings of the
Spiritual Heart practical and usable in our everyday lives

Contents

Foreword
From John Morton's Sharing
at Kenny's Memorial

Saturday, April 17, 2010

Kenny called it "The Grand Adventure."

I'd like to take this opportunity to speak on behalf of John-Roger, the founder of the Movement of Spiritual Inner Awareness and for myself as the spiritual director. Ken had a beautiful, tremendous dedication and love for this church for what it is preparing us to do. He demonstrated magnificently what coming to fulfillment is and what we are doing here in this beautiful, graceful relationship to the life of this world. And an open and complete embrace of the world to come.

During this last visit, I was with [my wife] Leigh, and Carol and Ken. It was a real opportunity to come to his view. In my experience, when a loved one is in transition, we have the opportunity to get close. Sometimes life being what it is, transition can sometimes be immediate and very sudden. And sometimes it can be gradual and full of opportunities to view, complete, and demonstrate what's going on deeply and profoundly. So I found out from both Ken and Carol about his deep love of nature and the natural world. In particular, he really loved tracking in the very most detailed and specific way, studying for many years. He was adept at going into nature and finding out what was there, how long it had been there—all kinds of creatures that might have passed.

I had the opportunity to take a tracking class when I was a park ranger. So I had a kinship with Ken in that way. Not that I in any way picked it up with discipline and application through life. But I realize the application joined in this is how to track the Spirit, and "soul nature" that we all have. In my view, Ken is going to leave us with a kind of legacy of how to do it full of grace, beauty, and the truth of who we are.

I already know it's working by how others have been bringing his touch and commenting deeply about how moved they are about the way he did his transition. I also was given, courtesy of Carol and her ministry to Ken, a view on how dedicated he was to taking care of himself. So he spent the last part of his life doing something very important to the teachings of this church, which is to take care of yourself. I consider he demonstrated how to do that with great mastery and exampleship—how to do everything possible to make the most out of living in this world.

He knew it was his time to embrace, and he really did that in a beautiful way, turning to the Spirit. Tracking into the Spirit. Telling us his human experiences. So I encourage you, if you are so inclined, to make some of his letters available to all. I don't know quite what to call them—sermons?—which express his view into the Spirit and his beautiful open embrace and surrender of his passing into the Spirit. One of the last things he told you, Carol, was that he needed you to not try to hang on but to let go. That was a demonstration of his consideration. He was very deeply committed to loving you and doing everything possible to be with you. Yet this is God's mystery to him, to make the passing in the time that God chooses.

This is God's mystery. Our view is that it's a perfect way. It's also a demonstration of perfection. But we can choose into this perfection so that it becomes something magnificent and beautiful to witness and be part of. I feel very thankful that I was part of his team called in to take part in witnessing what his view was.

He shared with me about his favorite movie, *Appaloosa*. So when we left our visit with Ken, Leigh and I watched *Appaloosa*. I had heard about the film but didn't know what it was really about. It's a western. It's an amazing story of friendship. It's based on the courage to say the truth even when it's not comfortable and not convenient and causes difficulties and challenges in this world.

Ken obviously demonstrated that as well as he worked John-Roger's definition of integrity, "Having the courage to go with the truth as you know it," and everything else that goes with that. So I'd like to do something that is my view into the Spirit.

When someone enters [the other side], and we're touched and connected as we are here today (and I'm sure as many others who are not here today), there is a blessing that is extended. As Spirit chooses its own, all are blessed.

So Lord, we ask for a special communion with Ken that comes in and from Spirit that we may all partake of the gifts of his presence, his life, and also extend in our way our love, our Light, our celebration for sharing in his life, and we extend whatever grace there is for his ongoing journey, and we know this is something that is also a great celebration in Spirit, the Beloved that is the Christ and those in this line of the Traveler.

Baruch Bashan [Hebrew for "the blessings already are"]

Preface
by Co-Author Ken Jones

November 23, 2011. One year, eight months, and three weeks after Kenny left his body, this message was received by co-author and wife, Carol Jones:

The purpose of this book from my point of view is Divine intervention. We are all divine, and until the moment of our death, we doubt that Divinity. From the plane on which I'm now living and looking, the human being is a direct emanation from soul, from the God Source, therefore Divine in every cell, every breath, even every thought, if one is willing to observe the root of the thought. The root of all thoughts, whether toxic or benevolent, is contained, surrounded, and embedded with living love.

In this book, the reader will find a personal blessing on every page, whether it is describing a perceived negative occurrence or a revelation of the Divine. The Lord God of the Universe oversees all levels of creation and loves them all. It is only believing our mind that leads us astray. My darling wife has given of her very nature in the outpourings on these pages. Read with an open mind and awareness of how your Spiritual Heart is responding. Therein lies the opportunity to make choices in alignment with your highest good. And so it will at once touch your loved ones whether they are aware of it or not. For every organism is connected to every other organism in the universe, and each one is contained within the whole—the Holy Spirit, the One God of the Universe.

By the way, I am, as we say on earth, "in blissful heaven." I am working hard, resting well, and contributing so much more than I could in my human body. And in case you're wondering, I spend time with Carol on a regular basis, mostly while she is sleeping. If you would like me to, I will be glad to make myself known to you also. Just ask inwardly for my presence (for the highest good of course—there is no imposition meant here).

I always remain a devoted student of the Holy Spirit, Carol's loving husband in Spirit, and your friend,

Ken Jones

Introduction

In June 2009, my husband, Ken Jones, was diagnosed with melanoma. Though we faced it with all the loving courage we could muster, researched endless "cures," and embarked on several in all earnestness and with a genuine sense of hope and openness to God's plan, he passed into Spirit on March 30, 2010.

Six months after Kenny passed, I received a message of indescribable comfort and infinite possibility: Kenny was still with me. *I love you,* he told me. *I am real. You can talk to me anytime.*

Everyone will pass from this world, and nearly everyone will have a loved one pass before them. It can be a glorious and Spirit-filled experience. In these pages, Kenny reveals how he did it, and I reveal the opening of my own heart in the process. *Through Kenny's Eyes* is an account of one soul's journey into conscious dying, the majesty of support he received from angels here on earth and on other realms, and one wife's experience of caring for him, grieving for him, and learning to experience his presence even after his body had gone from this world. I offer it for the upliftment of all those whose lives are touched by loss.

Messages from the Heart of God

In the days and weeks after Kenny passed, I prayed a lot that he would come to me with messages of wisdom, compassion, loving, and comforting. There were periods when my grief was so heavy on my heart and awareness that all I could do was recount the pain of my experiences.

Kenny and I studied the spiritual teachings of the Church of the Movement of Spiritual Inner Awareness (MSIA), founded by John-Roger, and we lived and worked at MSIA headquarters in Los Angeles along with other ministers and students. Throughout the nine months from when he was diagnosed to the day he stopped breathing, we took deep comfort in MSIA's core teachings about soul transcendence and how the different levels of consciousness function, our awareness of the Light that manifests divinity here in the physical world, and our shared, strong belief that in our essence, our "high form," we are one with God. Still, it wasn't until several months after Kenny passed that, for the first time since he passed, I put my hand to paper with the intention of contacting Kenny's soul.

Sometime in the summer of 2010, I made an appointment with Michael Hayes, a minister in MSIA who has the uncanny ability to see deeply into karmic patterns from this life and past existences. My intention for this session was to see if Michael could tell me how to reach Kenny's soul. His answer was based on the power of "intention." I sat with that for several more months, praying every night that Kenny would at least come to me in a dream, but not believing I could actually speak with him or hear him speak with me.

Then, in October of that year, I had the opportunity to meet with Saivahni, a dear friend who also, in her own unique way, sees and counsels from a perspective that includes the higher levels of consciousness. During lunch, she just happened to mention that I was a mental clairvoyant. I shrugged this comment off, feeling dense and impenetrable—after all, I could not sense Kenny's presence, nor could I hear his voice. And certainly I could not see him. He hardly ever came into my dreams, and when he did, I kept looking for him, never quite seeing him, losing him around every corner.

Saivahni tested me. She said, "Okay, what's the color of my aura?"

I said in disbelief and with a tone of resignation, "I have no idea!"

"Well, if you did know, what would it be?" Trick question meant to elicit truth. Ha, I thought. I offhandedly rattled off some colors.

Her response: "That's exactly right, and in the right order. I rest my case!"

Okay, so what's mental clairvoyance as opposed to any other kind? She explained that it's when intuition comes through the mental level of consciousness. The challenge—What is a message from the high realms? And what's just one of my thoughts? Trust in my intention, and God's direction will show the difference— that is the key teaching here.

Our next point of contact was a phone call in which Saivahni counseled me in reaching up to the highest level of consciousness I could, telling me that by intention and asking for my highest good to take place, the reaching actually could get me there. We asked for the presence of Spirit, and after giving me some words of encouragement through a kind of guided meditation, she asked me to say what I "heard." It wasn't exactly hearing that was going on; it was more phrases of thought, just like Saivahni had said about my ability as a mental clairvoyant. But what came through was so simple, so clear, and so pure that I was convinced it was not something my mind made up. Instead, my mind was simply being used as a vehicle for the message.

Here is what he said:

I'm with you more deeply now than ever before.
I have let go of everything in the way.
Come to me that way and uncover your own depth
of loving.
Let go...

*Kenny as a young man—I like envisioning
Kenny in his full vibrancy.*

Over the months that followed, more messages came, speaking of everything from the new realm of consciousness Kenny had entered to the practical matters of my daily life. And the letting go became more conscious, more palpable as it became more obvious that my response to life's challenges was changing for the better. The comfort Kenny's words provided soothed my aching heart. Imagine, he's asking me to meet him where he is, in the Spiritual Heart of God; he's telling me that that's where I'll find my healing, a voice for my grieving, the wisdom of my own past ages, and hope for the future.

As I thought about how to express the importance of this moment of receiving directly from Kenny's soul, I was reminded of a poignant prayer by John-Roger:

"As we reach up to our high form, we ask to be surrounded with the Light of the Christ. We ask for fulfillment and protection and only that which is the highest good of all concerned be brought forward. And we ask for this, Father, with love and understanding. So be it" (*Spiritual Exercises, Walking with the Lord* CD by John-Roger, Disc 2, Track 17).

What struck me so deeply in remembering this prayer was the notion of reaching up and contemplating the magnificence of my High Form or even *the* High Form, of God. With my innate visual focus, I could see myself reaching. I could see my High Form surrounded by the Light of the Christ. I could fill myself with the truth that if I ask, the Christ will fill not only me but any gap in experience or information I may need to fulfill my destiny. If I reach up, the Christ will meet me at the point of my action. How amazing is that! You'll see later in this book how this Christ action was so very important to Kenny's and my very existence as we skated over thin ice during those memorable days of treatment.

And today, as I reach up to my High Form where all high forms are one, I ask to be a clear channel for messages from Kenny's soul. I know that where my high form resides really is a realm of God consciousness, all knowing, peace and infinite love, where God has a place and a space for everyone and everything. Where all information, eons of history, and the spiritual wisdom schools and the ancient teachings exist, waiting for us to open our consciousness to receive of their glory.

Doubt creeps in from time to time as to my real abilities, but then I read back over the messages from Kenny, and I know they did not come from my mind or my own creativity. And I receive proof when I'm not even looking for it—as in this photograph that in earthly terms has no explanation.

Crosses and Ducks

The ducks are about two inches long and the crosses are about seven inches long. See how the crosses are perfectly aligned parallel to each other on the wooden surface and the ducks are all facing one direction? I did not place them in these positions. And no one else was in my room when I noticed how specifically they were placed. My only explanation is that Kenny somehow moved these objects to get my attention. It is widely known among those who study these matters that souls who have passed on are capable of "playing tricks" in just this way.

So on January 11, 2013, when I discovered this little tableau, I wrote my question to Kenny. Remember, the way I access these messages is through writing—I don't seem to be able to focus verbally or visually. So putting my hand to the task seems to keep me focused enough to get the message.

> Dearest Kenny,
> Did you move the ducks and the crosses?
> He responded
> Ahem—who else, my cutie pie!

So I am convinced that these messages come from that place way high in my consciousness where I am one with all there is. And "all there is" includes the Christ, the Mystical Traveler, God, my High Self, your High Self, all the Masters of Light that work with us, and so many more conscious beings, including Kenny's soul.

So while we could argue about just who's speaking through these messages, I am declaring they have value in their words of wisdom, unconditional loving, compassion, joy, and so much more of the soul's influence on us mortal beings here on Earth. And whether or not you believe there is such a thing as communication with our higher levels of consciousness, or with those souls who have dropped their bodies and gone on to higher realms of existence, I invite you to take from these messages the lessons and the healing that are available by applying the information to your own life (always, as we say in MSIA, keeping in mind the highest good of all concerned). Remember, Kenny said there is a blessing for each reader on every page.

On the other hand, if you must dismiss the messages as the ramblings of a grieving widow, that's fine with me too. Wherever you think they came from, know they have moved my consciousness through my memories, my experiences, and my lessons with grace and the unshakable inner knowing that I am in the right place at the right time doing the right thing. If I have learned nothing else from the experiences recounted in this book, I have learned and continue to learn one of the most challenging secrets of soul transcendence: that the only place to be is right here, right now! I have tiny inklings of the truth that all things are possible here and now. And as the days and weeks pass, those tiny inklings tickle my awareness more and more often. Nothing can be changed about the past, and both wishing we could change the past and ranging out to the future keep us from experiencing Spirit right here and now where all healing of memories exists, where all evolvement lies in wait.

"All I See Now Is Beauty"

In his life, Kenny was a tracker—an avid student of master tracker and wilderness teacher Tom Brown, himself a student of the Apache seer known as Grandfather. Tracking, simply put, is finding the significance in signs: examining scat to see where animals have passed; following trails to see where they lead; always asking, as Grandfather put it, the sacred question, "What does this mean?" *Why is this here? What can I learn from this? Where is my awareness lacking that this lesson had to be brought to me now?*

During his illness, Kenny turned that same scrutiny on everything that was happening to and for him. He started a blog to chronicle his treatments as well as the challenges and surprising pleasures of every day, and he explored his experience in countless thoughtful e-mails to friends, family, and our MSIA community. In the pages ahead, you'll read his blog posts—and some of mine—along with letters, e-mails, and responses from the many readers who followed his story with hope and love, before his passing and after. And of course, you'll continue to hear from Kenny as his blog ends and his communication shifts into its new form.

Kenny was also a photographer, and if you visit the book website www.throughkennyseyes.com, you'll see some of his magnificent nature photography. "All my work is of spiritual concern," he wrote while studying in the graduate program at the University of Florida. "[It] represents the interaction between a photographer and the light—a strange, mysterious, constantly changing, transforming light source that... changes the photographer as he tries to capture it." I hope you'll appreciate his acute sense of balance, of how light plays on his subject, how dimension reveals its far-reaching secrets, and how, as the seer expressing his soul's love of Earth's bountiful beauty, he surrounded himself with the sights and sounds of the vast and varied American wilderness.

And I hope you'll take in the essence of something I have sometimes struggled to describe adequately in words: the oneness of purpose Kenny and I felt as we moved forward together to support his healing. Driven, selfless, dedicated, and devoted. Tireless, fed by Spirit. Consciously following Spirit's lead. As the book progresses, this is expressed in many different ways, in our daily interactions and deep reflections, as well as in quotes and messages from John-Roger, the founder of MSIA, and John Morton, its spiritual director. Ken and I were devoted initiates and ministers in this teaching, finding deep inspiration in the practice and everyday simplicity of this work. Now I continue the challenges of completing karma in this life while Kenny's soul does its work in the realms unseen.

Of his teacher, tracker Tom Brown, wrote, "The truth, the simple truths of life, was what Grandfather was seeking. His seeking many times would lead him to the edge of death, but it was at this edge that the most profound lessons would be learned. Many times this was the only way they could be learned." For Kenny, too, the edge of death was a place of dazzling discovery.

"I take meds to control my pain, and I handle the basic body functions to keep it going, and my consciousness dances free in the Light of God," he said in his blog not long before he died. "I feel as though I am among the 'Living Free.' I have so little standing between me and the awareness of God that practically all I see is beauty."

And that is the reason I am compelled to share our story: so this book may give you a glimpse of that beauty, as seen *Through Kenny's Eyes*.

Refer to the Glossary for explanations of terms and Resources for Further Study.

Chapter 1

Big Time to Focus Up

Ken, July 7, 2009

Hello, my beloved family,

My diagnosis came back as metastatic malignant melanoma cancer in my liver and spleen and in some lymph nodes in between, plus a few small nodes in my lungs and bones. The tumors are too numerous to treat with surgery or radiation, so I'm probably looking at some form of chemotherapy or immunotherapy in the near future. I hope it will be immunotherapy. I have consulted with two of the top oncologists in LA, melanoma specialists, and have discussed a variety of treatments. It looks like a challenging road ahead, so I am learning all I can and constantly looking for the blessings in my situation. There are many. It's a very focusing time of my life. I am taking in all the opinions of the experts and weighing them to choose the course of treatment that will be for my highest good and the highest good of all concerned.

I have wonderful support from Carol and my Prana family (MSIA Headquarters), so that is very comforting. It has been nine years since I had melanoma surgery on my shoulder, and my doctors are encouraged by how slowly the tumors have been growing and that I still have no symptoms. I wouldn't have even known I had cancer if I hadn't gone to the emergency room (on my sister, Genia's birthday) to check out what I thought was a blocked intestine.

On another note, this past week was the annual MSIA conference where people come from all over the world to celebrate and spend time together. There was a two-day workshop (Heartfelt Service), followed by a wonderful dinner and entertainment. I was part of the international fashion show. I went as a flirty Ukrainian woman named Pickup Andropov, whose service is foot massage, only she massages people with her feet. According to many people, my act was a big hit.

Kenny as Pickup Andropov at the MSIA
Conference of Service July 2009
Photo used with permission from MSIA.

Yesterday, we had an all-day event/fundraiser here at Prana called The Blessingsfest, and I was fortunate to attend. Each participant received a card on which to write what blessings they want. Then John Morton, spiritual director of MSIA, read each card aloud and talked about the subject a bit. Of course I asked for good health. There were many messages in the whole event for me, and I was very uplifted by it.

I will send you all new information as it shows up. Please pray for my full recovery and picture me living another thirty years.

I love you all very much. We have had a wonderful time together so far, and I want to keep sharing the good times with you for many years to come.

Chapter 2

Kenny Warms up to What's Really Going On

Ken, December 9, 2009

Hi, folks,

This is my first blog, and it's about my challenges with melanoma cancer.

Food

Have been on the infamous Gerson Therapy (GT) in some form since mid-July. It is composed of all-organic vegetables and fruits, mostly in the form of fresh-pressed juices. While on the full GT, I was consuming about twenty pounds of veggies and fruits a day.

While full GT calls for thirteen juices a day, now, because of the internal bleeding, my therapy calls for only seven juices a day: two carrot, three apple-carrot, and two green juices.

While full GT calls for both raw and cooked food in the lunch and dinner, now I am only eating cooked food at both lunch and dinner, due to my duodenal ulcer. We were afraid that raw food would irritate it too much. Because the workload is large with GT, we hired a domestic helper to do the juicing, prepare the food, and do other household chores. This has been a great help..

Meds

I'm taking Dexamethasone to reduce the swelling of the tumors in my brain. It causes the excess fluid to accumulate in my feet instead. My feet are swollen from toes to knee and have prickly, old-man skin.

I'm taking Oxycodone to mask the pain of melanoma consuming my body like a bunch of rats that just found used cheesecloth.

I'm taking omeprazole to buffer the stomach acid so I can eat even while having a bleeding ulcer in my duodenum. There may be other bleeding places along the digestive system. My oncologist seems to think so.

I'm also taking Novotiral, which is a Mexican brand of thyroid meds.

Melanoma

Each day brings a new challenge. Carol, my saint of a wife, and I have been exceptionally resourceful at meeting those challenges. It helps that we live among many beautiful friends here at Peace Awareness Labyrinth and Gardens near downtown Los Angeles.

Kenny on the Beach at Baja Nutri Care Clinic

Kenny in his hero outfit as Indiana Jones

Detoxing

Each day, I do two coffee enemas, 6:00 a.m. and 6:00 p.m. This detoxifies my liver and keeps it functioning. Yesterday morning I had a blood draw and got the report yesterday afternoon. It showed my liver and kidneys functioning normally. Without the enemas, which are central to the Gerson Therapy, my liver couldn't survive the flood of toxins the melanoma is pouring into my bloodstream.

I get so much pleasure and overall body relief from the enemas that I look forward to each one with delightful anticipation. It's one of my favorite parts of the day.

—Esther Jantzen—

> I am thrilled that you are writing about this experience, Ken. I know you to be a committed adventurer and tracker, and perhaps you're in a woods or forest of a different kind now, tracking your way through and out. I see you could be a guide and teacher for many others.

> It was Esther who encouraged Kenny to start this blog. Thank you from both of us, Esther. What a gift it has been.

—Cousin Emilie—

> Bless you for sharing your story. I will be praying for you this Ash Wednesday in our school chapel service. The elementary school children at Episcopal Day School in Pensacola have great power in their prayer.
> Hugs,
> Emilie

In a message from Kenny on November 5, 2010, seven months and six days after he passed, he explains how the melanoma gained entrance into his body.

My darling Kenny, are you with me today?

Always, my love.

Why did you leave?

It was meant to be. I could have made some other choices earlier, but I bet against my odds and couldn't sustain the trauma of my life pattern. Yes, it was set up in childhood when I dared to break out, but was so compelled to secret that it took great energy away from my immune system. So that, coupled with the environmental toxicity, led to a breakdown in systems.

My darling, please go forward. Don't keep second guessing the past. Just learn to go forward without guilt. There is no blame. I love you now more than ever because my pure soul reaches into your heart and fills you with encouragement, fulfillment and pleasure. Seek the joy in compiling the work. Use everything I have written and captured on film.

God blesses you, my sweetie, just like I do.
I love you eternally,
Kenny

Chapter 3

Our Spiritual Teachers Took Every Step with Us

Carol, September 14, 2009, message to John-Roger and John Morton

Beloved J-R and John,

This is just a note to update you on the Gerson Therapy Ken is undergoing—and I am to a certain extent also. I am not doing the full therapy but modified for a "healthy" person. I just saw the same cornea specialist I saw two years ago when I had that very serious infection in my left eye. He stuck with me long enough to see improvement. When we were over the hump, he confided that he had been afraid I'd lose the eye. Whatever part you played in this miracle, I am eternally grateful. As a result of the Gerson protocol, my eyesight improved and my astigmatism disappeared.

As for sweet Kenny, he has been having some pretty strong healing reactions. This is what the doctors are looking for, as scary as they are—a lot of pain and pressure in his abdomen, a persistent cough and pain where he damaged some rib cartilage the first day he was in Mexico. These healing reactions are pretty scary for both of us, but we are in close contact with the doctors in Mexico and they, plus the books and paperwork they gave us, give us things to do for pain like the "pain triad"— Advil, vitamin C, and niacin—clay packs, castor oil packs, hot water bottles, peppermint tea, oatmeal gruel, and more enemas to flush out the toxins the body is trying to get rid of. Kenny is such a brave patient. He's doing everything right. But when he's in pain, I become a basket case, tearing up and crying. I do pull myself together and assist as best I can, but I do need to clear my emotions (fear/panic) often to stay helpful.

Thank you for all you, the Traveler, are doing for us, and for your personal interest in his progress. We are so grateful to have the Traveler working with us, and to all the wonderful friends who are helping. And to Virginia Rose, whom we are paying to juice on weekdays, Ana Isabel, whom we are paying to do laundry and clean the bedroom, and to a good number of volunteers who are assisting us, including Ross Goodell doing prayer communion almost every night and Tatiana Jimenez joining him sometimes.

Residents at Prana and administration have been so generous in letting us use the scullery to make the juices and order foods that we need. We're grateful for every gesture of kindness.

We love you and feel closer than ever to your love.

Carol

John-Roger and John Morton's correspondence secretary writes:

Dear Carol,

I sent your letter to J-R and John, and John had some responses. You brought them up to date on Ken's situation and its effect on you, and you wrote, "I cry every day and feel ineffective in helping him lift his consciousness to that place of hope and conviction or whatever it is that will move him into survival and beating the cancer." You asked how you can best minister to Ken, and John encouraged you to love in the ways that nurture and heal, including with yourself first.

John also said he does understand your wanting to do all you can to encourage Ken's long life and healing. And it is still his to do, between him and God. You can assist, but if you have any feelings that you are responsible for his healing and survival, it's best to let those go. He is going through his own karma, and that is the important thing, and from the Soul's perspective, there is nothing wrong. And when you find yourself being upset, worried, etc., and think you shouldn't be, you can forgive yourself for judging yourself. It's never easy to see a loved one in pain, and you have your own karma in the situation. So focus on what you can learn, what you yourself can clear and bring from fear into loving, how you can love yourself more, how you can attune more to Spirit. And sometimes karma is cleared (lessons are learned) by simply going through a situation, no matter how a person does that. And John said, he is with you both.

You also wrote, "I know Ken is one of yours and ultimately you have him already no matter what is going on in the physical." John said that's right, and you are one of the Traveler's, too.

Love,
Betsy

Chapter 4

Indiana Jones and the Temple of Love

The article that follows, published in the March 2010 issue of the *New Day Herald*, is a comprehensive explanation from Ken about how Spirit is working with him, how he experiences the cancer in his body, and how impactful our community and our personal relationship effects his outlook on his condition and his life.

Ken, February 7, 2010

Yesterday, my good buddy Kevin McMillan interviewed me for an article in the *New Day Herald,* and David Sand took pictures. The NDH is the newspaper for the Movement of Spiritual Inner Awareness (MSIA). MSIA is an organization dedicated to teaching and facilitating Soul Transcendence while here in the physical body.

Kevin and David came to my room, and Kevin asked me some basic questions to help get me going. I had a good time with Kevin, as usual. Other than Carol, Kevin is my best friend.

The New Day Herald Article
"Indiana Jones and The Temple Of Love"
Interview with Ken Jones
by Kevin McMillan

Kenny shares candidly with Kevin McMillan.
Photo used with permission from MSIA.

KM: So, Ken, I've known you a long time. Helen Bradley and I picked you up at the airport when you first moved to Prana fifteen years ago.

KJ: That's right.

KM: At which time, I don't know if you remember, but we predicted that you might be a good match for Carol.

KJ: [Laughs] I heard about that! Yeah, I flew in from Kauai where I'd been living for six years, when I found out about the (PTS) master's program, and I said wow, that's for me! So I called up and applied, got accepted for the master's, and then

I found out that if you're a Prana resident you can take the master's for free. This was a time when the construction was going on after the Northridge earthquake, and there was a lot of noise and dust, and clamor, and people—you know living at Prana wasn't very popular then—so it was pretty easy to get accepted as a resident. Then I had to get rid of a whole lot of stuff so I could move, and came with a great big shipping crate full of my old stuff, and put it down there on the basketball court, and moved in. Moved in right across the hall from Carol, and no, I didn't know that you were doing matchmaking, but I was doing my own matchmaking, and so was she. Because I was casting a hook out there, saying man, I've had a bunch of relationships that haven't worked out, I want a Soul Initiate, it's time… everything else I'll take, but I want a Soul Initiate. So, that's what I put out, and we discovered each other.

KM: And then how long later did you guys marry?

KJ: A little more than a year. As part of my (Prana) church service, I had to volunteer, so I chose three different paths to check out and see what I wanted to do. And one of them was assisting Carol with her PTS work. I'd go down to her office a couple of nights a week for a couple of hours and started creating some custom databases. I would assist her doing her work, so we got to have a lot of conversations, and got to know each other, and heck—it was just the following month, wasn't it Carol? at Thanksgiving—after the Thanksgiving meal, which we both helped prepare, we went into the large seminar room with everyone else to watch a movie, it was something like *Little Buddha*, and we sat next to each other and held hands. And that was the first time we expressed any affection for each other. That's when we started dating, and that was I guess our first date. But anyway, that was how that relationship got started.

KM: And then I remember I sang at your wedding at Prana.

KJ: Yep.

KM: And you and I come from towns in South Carolina about thirty miles away from each other, but we never knew each other until Prana.

KJ: That's right.

KM: And now we're continuing the journey. So I've known you a long time, and right now I'd say that you seem more radiant and clear, and loving and balanced, than I've probably ever seen you.

KJ: I'd say that's true as well. This has been a time for consciousness as well as physical clearing, and cleansing and purging and forgetting and forgiving, and letting go and loving unconditionally. All that's been going on. So it is indeed fantastic—not just a blessing—but the answer to a lifelong prayer, to clean out and get with what's real, and be the spiritual being that I am, the divine soul that I am. I've said those words before, but now it's coming from a place of realness and conviction. I know that's it, because the rest of the crap's pretty much gone. [Laughs.] Every day is just so beautiful, and I'm so grateful.

KM: So what would you like people to know about what you're going through right now?

KJ: My change of life started back in June [2009] when I had a stomach pain and went to the emergency room on my doctor's advice, and found out the melanoma that I had to have surgery for back in 2000 had come back and metastasized through quite a few of my internal organs. It was a shock and a surprise. Melanoma's a very aggressive type of cancer, and very deadly usually, so the doctors wanted to do some further scans and tests, and found out that that's indeed what it was, and suggested that

I'd better get chemotherapy starting tomorrow. Well, somehow I had already found out that chemotherapy doesn't work with metastasized melanoma. All it does is over-tox the liver and kill you. I mean, it does reduce the tumors temporarily, but it gives you maybe one or two months' more life, that you supposedly wouldn't have had if you hadn't done the chemo. They said surgery and radiation were out of the question, so the only option was chemo. But that's partly because those are the only three legal options doctors can offer in California anyway, so I didn't have any other choice, and they don't know anything else.

I had a friend who advised me to look into Gerson Therapy, which is based on hyper-nutrition and detoxification through organic vegetable juices. You bring the body hyper-nutrition, and drive the toxins out of the cells and into the bloodstream, and then use coffee enemas to allow the toxins that collect in the liver to flush out on a daily basis. Keeps the liver healthy. I just did a blood test yesterday. My liver and kidney functions are almost normal, and I'm here into... this is the seventh month I guess, and I don't have any neurological symptoms, although I do have brain tumors. The melanoma's gone into my brain, and heart, and lungs, and digestive system, and who knows where else it could be? And I'm suspecting that it's in my prostate; I know it's in the gall bladder too, ribs, pelvis, and one other... can't remember the other organ—but there's another one affected right now as well. So it's kind of a race for time.

KM: I've been seeing you pretty regularly the last few weeks, and just from the outside, I don't see you in a lot of discomfort. Of course I'm sure there could be times that I'm just not seeing it, but is there much pain?

KJ: No pain.

KM: No pain?

KJ: No pain. My oncologists are quite puzzled, not only by why I'm still alive, but why I'm not in pain, why I'm not suffering, why I can still stand up and walk around, have a good time talking to people, and be pretty much functional. How is this possible? Well, in my opinion it's the Gerson Therapy that's keeping me alive right now, but it looks like, in spite of the Gerson—which has benefited me tremendously—the melanoma is still the overriding thing going on, and it'll eventually take me down if I don't do anything differently; through seizures, or a heart attack, or something like that.

So, you know, facing that very real prospect, I've had tremendous counseling, and blessing and comforting from John Morton—and J-R— but John Morton has personally addressed my situation several times, and reminded me that what's the big deal, we're all taken care of by the Traveler anyway, and everybody's going to let go of their body at some time or another, in some way or another. It's temporary, baby, for everybody! So you just let it go and you go into God's arms with the guidance and protection of the Traveler, and you float into the Soul Realm, and hey—there you are, baby, in a better place. So there's nothing to fear. For me, death has no more fear than going to sleep. You just let it go, and you go into something that's, well… here is very limiting, and constricted, and challenging, and requires constant vigilance and resourcefulness. And you move from that into a place where there's this huge expansion of peace and joy and love, and wow, who wouldn't want to do that? So there's no fear here at all, and I'm just enjoying every day to the maximum, and so grateful for all the love and the support, and good cheer, and the blessings and the Light and love that people are sending me in all kinds of ways. And I'm just soaking it in. It's really fantastic, and of course it's a fantastic blessing to be living here at Prana, Peace Awareness Labyrinth and Gardens, where the energy is the best on the planet in terms of quality and purity of Light and upliftment and, wow!

KM: So what would you say to others who might be diagnosed with a similar condition?

KJ: Seek all the alternatives, and take full responsibility for your own therapy, your own course of therapy, your own well-being, your own state of health. Listen to the doctors, listen to the alternative practitioners, gather information, but make your own decisions. Don't let any of them take authority over your health. That's what I did, and I'm so glad, and so blessed. I have orthodox doctors, and I have alternative doctors, and practitioners, and friends who are always suggesting things that might help, but I'm making the decisions about how I do this. And it's a strength-building thing to do that. There are plenty of doctors who are curing cancer out there without chemo and radiation and surgery.

I will be attending the Burzynski clinic starting soon for two weeks [February 8] in Houston, Texas, where they're doing advanced genetic research to clear cancer from the body, all kinds of cancer. They conduct FDA-approved clinical trials for this, so it's all kosher as long as they stay within certain guidelines and do certain protocols. But the main thing is that this Dr. Stanislaw Burzynski has come up with a way to alter the genetic makeup of the body, to replace genetic parts that are missing in cancer patients, and to remove parts of the genetic makeup that are causing the cancer. He calls it Antineoplaston Therapy, which is just a big word he made up that means anti-cancer. It has to do with modifying peptides and proteins into certain forms, first with injectable medicines to identify your proper course of therapy, and then once they get that course set, they give you oral pills to take home, and check in with you once a month for three months, and make sure things are working and you're on course. It's very expensive, but fortunately we're able to do it at this time. We're very excited about it, and we'll be flying out Monday morning with as much of our clinical gear as we can hide in our bags. [smiles] My bedroom's sort of turned into a mini-clinic here. But we have the fantastic blessing of the assistance of HeartReach, which is assisting us in setting up volunteers in Houston, in the church, who will be doing this very valuable task for us—shopping, cooking, and juicing for us while we're there. A friend in the Dallas-Fort Worth area is putting that all together, and coordinating it for us. It's such a fantastic service that she's doing for us, because it's a lot of work, and it would be overwhelming for Carol to try to handle that and all of my immediate needs as well.

KM: Speaking of Carol, I know that she's been an amazing source of love and support for you. What's it like to have that kind of love and support?

KJ: Wow. Beyond anything I had thought could be. I'd heard about unconditional loving, heard J-R talk about it many times, and thought about it, and attempted it. And what I see every day is Carol demonstrating it. And I mean to the point where she wants to take care of me and make me well so much that—I don't know—sometimes it's hard to take it all in, but I'm working on that. The Loving Each Day (daily e-mail quotes from John-Roger or John Morton; visit http://www.msia.org/subscribe to sign up or for more information) today talked about loving each other 100 percent in a relationship, and I see her doing that, day after day after day, loving me 100 percent. And I told her today, well I hope I am doing the same for her, and if I'm not I'm certainly going to be looking for ways to bump my percent up to 100 for her as well. So it's the sweetest, most caring, most caressing, supportive… she gives me the feeling that she would do anything to take care of me. She goes shopping, she prepares food, she tucks me into bed at night, she washes me, she gives me showers in the morning. I mean it is phenomenal what Carol has been expressing, and coordinating paid workers as well as volunteers to help us do everything possible to keep me healthy in the physical body so we can spend more time together. It's amazing.

Carol and Ken during the interview
Photo used with permission from MSIA.

KM: It's a beautiful ministry.

KJ: It really is.

KM: And in my perception your relationship is just so sweet these days.

KJ: It is.

KM: Speaking of taking care of your body, I know you've lost a lot of weight. I wanted to ask, has the relationship to your body and the way that you see yourself and your body changed?

KJ: Well somewhat, you know, I can't help when I look in the mirror to see I've lost sixty pounds. The melanoma is eating up my skeletal muscle, so each day it becomes a little more challenging to stand up and walk, because I get weaker. So that's why it's kind of a race against time to get to the Burzynski Clinic and get this therapy going, so we can reverse that and I can start, you know, exercising and building muscle back. It's not like I can't do it. When I was fourteen I had an operation on both knees. They put me in a wheelchair for a month, and my muscles atrophied at that time, and I lost all the muscle tone. At the end of that period, when I first stood up out of the wheelchair and tried to walk, I could only walk across the room and sit down. So it was starting almost from scratch, learning how to walk, and not just the muscles but how to coordinate them. And it was a proud day when I stood up and walked across the room. And this would be very much the same, once the cancer's in remission, which in Burzynski happens pretty quickly. I can start building my muscle back, and get my strength back, so I'm looking forward to that. But it does affect my body image. Is that what you're asking?

KM: Well, this may be just a projection, but I was thinking about this to ask you today. I know that for me, when I was in the hospital a while back, and I wasn't feeling well, and I was looking really pale and not well and had lost some weight, I just got the sense that I'm really not my body—that became really clear to me.

KJ: Oh yeah!

KM: That the body's just a vehicle.

KJ: Right, exactly. It's like when I stand up to walk, I'm aware that I'm walking something other than what I am. I'm directing something almost like from above, you know, okay now we're going to make the legs walk, you remember how to do that don't you? You swing your arms, that's right, let's get it coordinated.

KM: Like a marionette.

KJ: Yeah like a marionette, yeah definitely [Laughs].

KM: We always hear about living here and now. A lot of philosophies talk about that. You told me at one point that because of certain factors in your condition, the doctors have told you that there was a potential that something could rupture... that you could pass away at any time.

KJ: Right.

KM: So what's it like living moment to moment, day to day like that?

KJ: You just take every moment as it comes. It's almost like being in combat, where there's bullets flying at you, and you don't know whether one's going to hit you or not, and even if one hits you, you may not know it. You just go on, you know? I watch these things on TV that show people being shot at, and I think, *That guy acts like it's not bothering him.* And I thought, *Well, that's what this is like.* That I could have an instant medical event—a physical event that takes me out—and again, so what? Big deal. You just relax and let go, and there's the Traveler, and you go.

KM: And really anybody could have that, it's just there's more of an awareness of it.

KJ: Not just an awareness, but a probability of it with me, rather than somebody getting hit by a bus walking out the front of Prana or something. That's low probability, but my probability is high that I'll be taken out soon, quickly. So that's there to contemplate, but I don't spend any time thinking about that. Big deal. That's a waste of time.

KM: It seems like you're just being grateful for the day and for right now. I notice you've been doing a lot of, well... [laughs] some shopping online, and getting some things that you like, ordering some awesome clothes, and collecting authentic handmade replicas of American Indian items.

KJ: Right! [Laughter.] You see that? I got that bark quiver. It's an exact replica of one that's in the Smithsonian, and handmade arrows, to go with the archery bow that I carved from a piece of wood, and my darts, and yeah... having fun! My Indiana Jones outfit, my western outfit, and we just ordered custom-made cowboy hats.

KM: Oh, that's so cool! Are you going to have them in Texas?

KJ: Yeah, they're going to send them to us on Valentine's Day, and then we'll wear them when we come back too.

KM: Is there anything you'd like people to know about the best way to deal with, or relate to, somebody with a situation like yours?

KJ: Well in my case, most people are very open and loving and glad to see me, and it's such a treat but, sometimes I see people looking at me like they don't want to talk to me, or they want to avoid me, because I look so different. In fact, most people don't recognize me at first now.

KM: Oh really?

KJ: We bumped into some friends at the co-op, and they didn't recognize me the first instant, and then, "Oh, it's you!"—you know, that kind of thing. So I don't look at myself as some sort of invalid, and I don't like it when people look at me that way. I don't like that image because I don't feel crippled in any way.

I feel whole. And just because my body's going through some challenges, that's not who I am. So it's better to have people just treat me like a regular person and have a conversation with me.

I had the great delight recently to have a friend who's a doctor bring his family over and spend an hour with me, letting me talk about my process. He wanted his kids to see somebody who has a dangerous form of cancer, and how I'm dealing with it, perhaps quite differently from other people. And that was a treat. I loved to be of service that way. I decided that there's not much I can do in terms of my ministry other than bringing the Light and the love and the joy into people's lives the best way I can. And one way is to share like that with people about my condition, my process. Obviously my brain function isn't suffering, my memory, my speech patterns, or any of those neurological things, so I can carry on a clear, consistent conversation with people. That's partly because of the meds I'm on, and partly because of the Gerson Therapy. To allow me to focus on the joy that I have in my life right now, and to express that to people, is just such a treat, a blessing. My gift. [crying] My ministry.

KM: What a beautiful example of that.

KJ: Thank you. [crying]

KM: And I really see you being a spiritual warrior.

KJ: I am. I'm a spiritual warrior I'm discovering, you know? I'm living the spiritual fulfillment that J-R promises, and I know that it's not complete in any way, but it's the process, and I'm going through it, and I'm discovering the inexpressible joy that goes with that unfoldment. And I can see, when I do my spiritual exercises [s.e.'s] and I chant my initiation tone, it's like I realized this morning there's a door in front of me with sort of spinning poles, and I have to get my poles spinning at the same rate as that door in front of me in order to go through it with my tone. That's why I do my tone, I have to bring my rate up with my tone to match the doorway that the Traveler's holding open for me to get into the Soul Realm. And so I just do it, and it's so simple and innocent. I just say my tone and it happens. It's like magic! I don't understand it—but, man, that feeling is from chanting my tone and I'm there, and I know when I'm there with the Traveler, and that I'm matching that energy and I'm going into it. But I just need to do it more, more s.e.'s, more s.e.'s. [Laughs]

KM: Like J-R says, more *s.e.*'s. [Both laugh]

KJ: So, Mr. Jones, just a couple more questions. Number one is, you seem to be getting better looking—How can that be?

KJ: Well, it's part of the physical clearing-out process, there's an age regressing factor that starts coming into play, and you get younger and younger, and your skin clears up, and your wrinkles disappear, you just become more and more beautiful, to the point where I have to wear sunglasses to look in the mirror! [Lot of laughter]

KM: Can I quote you on that?

KJ: You may! It's dazzling, I have to say!

KM: It's good to be the king. So the last question. It's been just great to talk to you here, so what is it you'd like people to know about your life and who you are?

KJ: Oh, that's an interesting question, sort of like an epitaph? Let's see. Well, you know, I could say I'm a loving person, a divine soul who's enjoying every moment of life. I've learned not to take anything for granted; simplest things can bring great pleasure, and you may not want to put this in the article, but just being able to get up at night and pee, and get back in bed. There are people who can't do that, and I am really grateful I can, and so you know simple things make a huge difference. Let's see. I am the eternal optimist. I see myself going to this clinic in Texas and clearing my body, not just bringing it back to a state of health but with an entirely raised vibration, almost like ready for the induction of a higher form of consciousness to come into this body that's been so purified and cleansed, and you know, with no toxins or anything like that in it. So I see myself coming out of this healthier than ever before.

KM: Well, I'm excited for you.

KJ: Thank you.

KM: Thank you for sharing. I really love you.

KJ: I love you too, and I really appreciate all the loving things, and the fun that we've had, and the service that you've provided me in various ways, and it's been a real treat, and a real intimate friend that I really cherish, and it's been great. South Carolina buddies!

KM: Okay, God bless you.

KJ: God bless you too.

Kevin and Kenny
Photo used with permission from MSIA

Carol's letter published in the May 2010 issue of the *New Day Herald*

Dear MSIA family,

The January issue of the *New Day Herald* contained a beautiful interview with my sweetheart and husband, Kenny Jones, about his journey with Spirit and metastasized malignant melanoma cancer. The story was less about the cancer and much more about his spiritual awakening and his conscious life with the Traveler. Some of you may not know that after some of the most joy-filled days of his life, he passed into Spirit on March 30, 2010.

He told me he was happy. He had everything he needed. He relished the simple things like his daily baths, good food, loving friends who came to visit, and HeartReach's Circle of Light. The sacred tones and his adoring wife at his side, he was ready to let go of the body. My sweetheart showed us how to make our final transition from this world in grace and with dignity, joy, humor, and fun.

As for those of us still here on planet earth, he would be very grateful (and so would I) if you would share his blog with as many people as possible so the folks out there can see for themselves that at least one trailblazer did it consciously and with great love for humankind. I continue to make entries to the blog whenever I realize what I am experiencing would help someone else.

My thanks, and I know he would thank you as well, for all the prayers worldwide, the cards and seeds, your presence at his bedside and his memorial service and your physical help, and the tenderness and love you are extending to me.

God bless us all on our journey back to the heart of God.

With Love, Light, and Gratitude,

Carol

Our dear friend, poet Robert Peake, laments his son's early passing. In this poem he also talks about Ken's writing (New Posts/Short Books, Lost Horse Press, 2011, also published in the *New Day Herald*).

"Koi Pond"
In memoriam of KJ

I went to pay a visit to the koi,
To see what they thought of my life,
And how I had been living it.
Beneath the imperturbable surface,
They mouthed the words, saying
"bleb" and "bleb" and "bleb."
Some torpedoed, others swung
A lazy fin, like an oarsman,

Turning a casual arc. Some lay
Like unexploded mines, chin up.
I became so outwardly still,
The black cat crossing the painted
red bridge failed to notice me,
and the turtle drifted shoreward
like a sail with six points.
Of course, my son, who lived
too briefly for my liking,
was there with me as well,
and my pocket notebook held
against my hip many small
laments, carefully arranged.
A friend of mine is writing
about his melanoma, having reached
bemused indifference that he
could go at any time, hoping
for more life, and smiling
like a child at his future.
What is the future, koi, who
sip the rare pond surface,
and descend? You are here
to teach me something, I am
sure, just like the tumors
in the dark organs, blooming.
And when our pediatrician
bowed his head, that man
of science became ordained
a priest of human religion.
What was his prayer again?
The water going dark only
makes the orange seem brighter,
as you race, and kiss, and spar
for food, pretending not
to notice me. For this gift

of your indifference, I am
grateful. I will sit until
the pond goes black, the last
orange spark extinguished.

LOVING EACH DAY

REFLECTIONS ON THE *S* PIRIT WITHIN

Graphic used with permission from MSIA

Spirit will never give you anything you can't handle. So you can be assured that you will always be able to handle what is. You do that by staying present in the moment and just moving through each experience as it appears. Those of you who work with the Mystical Traveler Consciousness know that I go through these things with you. You are never alone. You are perfectly protected at all times. And as you become more aware and trusting of that process, life can become very joyful.

—John-Roger, The Way Out Book

Chapter 5

The Burzynski Clinic

Ken, February 8, 2010

Today, Carol and I are flying Continental Airlines to Houston, Texas, to start two weeks of cancer treatment at the Burzynski Clinic and research facility.

Dr. Stanislaw Burzynski has been doing leading edge, one-of-a-kind genetic research on cancer patients through FDA-approved clinical trials using antineoplastons. Antineoplastons are modified peptides or proteins that have the ability to turn off oncogenes (cancer-causing genes) and others that turn on tumor-suppressor genes (kills cancer cells).

Tomorrow we go for my first consultation with the clinic, and we are exhausted from travel, but excited.

Our accommodations in Houston couldn't be more perfect. We are staying at the Candlewood Suites Hotel, also known locally as the "Burzynski Hotel." No ownership implied. A large part of the perfection of it is due to Carol's skill at getting what she wants through planning and coordinating the future. In this case, she did it sight unseen, through faith and working with the Divine Light of God.

Day 1

We are here in Dr. Burzynski's clinic, in his conference room, waiting for the good doctor himself. His clinic is very big, modern, and impressive. I found out today that I will be here for targeted gene therapy instead of antineoplaston clinical trials. I did *not* qualify for the antineoplaston clinical trials because they are reserved for patients whose brain tumors originated in the brain. My brain tumors are secondary, meaning they are an extension of the melanoma metastasizing in the brain.

The clinic has been behind schedule since we arrived by at least a half-hour. I got very annoyed at one point but realized that since we have asked Spirit for the highest good to take place, there's nothing to worry about.

We met with the famous Dr. Burzynski and his team at the clinic. The clinic itself is very impressive, all modern, glassy, big, new, and humming along inside with the almost all Polish personnel. I got some photos.

I had my consultation, physical exam, and blood draw with Dr. Burzynski's team today and scheduled tomorrow's appointments with Houston Medical Imaging for the PET scan with contrast and an echocardiogram. Then back to the Burzynski Clinic for my appointment with a doctor on his staff.

Day 2

It's very cold in Houston today, overcast. Jesus Ordonez came early, brought Pedialyte so I can stay hydrated, and helped out tremendously getting us ready for the day with juices, food, cleaning, and even helping me get my shower. What an angel!

The PET scan was delayed by more than an hour, and because I couldn't eat or drink anything during that time, I got dehydrated and tired. I had the echocardiogram first. The tech was sweet and efficient. I'm waiting at Houston Medical

Imaging center to get my PET scan. They injected me with the radioactive stuff about half an hour ago. Now it's time to take my Oxycodone with a sip of water.

Sleep

Sleep is of prime importance yet it eludes me, particularly at night. It's like I want to avoid that which would be most beneficial for me. Aha! The death wish.

Our trip was exhausting, and we are both struggling to get enough sleep and rest to catch up. I am staying hydrated but not rested. We may have to cut short part of our visit today in order to get back on our critical schedule.

(See chapter 8: The Edge, for the latest update on sleep.)

Lord God, once again we give thanks for the opportunity to be with You. We ask that You bring us forward from whatever we have chosen that would keep us lagging or restricted from knowing You.

Lift us from our pretenses and falsehoods that we have placed before ourselves as judgments and false knowledge. We ask that You take away the illusion and that You may assist us, regardless of what we have done.

We come to You in grace, to the door of forgiveness. Restore our joy and courage, that we can go through each day and whatever meets us, knowing the blessings of each moment and being glad in what we behold as eternal truth.

We bring our enthusiasm to do the best we can. We trust that You are always with us and that You have prepared the way.

There is nothing against us that will ever last. Whatever negativity we find shall not prevail. We are resurrected in the Christ. The Holy Spirit is our companion.

You bring the Lord's hand to touch us, strength to lift us, vision to look upon Your face, Light to let us see the truth, and wisdom to know that Your will is done. And we find everlasting peace in Your loving embrace.

—John Morton, *You Are the Blessings*

Chapter 6

The Death Wish

Ken, February 9, 2010

The death wish was the prime unconscious motivating factor in the development of my cancer.

My death wish had both the standard manifestation as well as at least one unexpected alternative interpretation. The standard one simply said, "Get me out of here! I can't handle this world. It's too harsh and cruel. I don't understand it, nor can I control it. It's not fair. It's too painful."

And yet I'm too timid to just kill myself. Suicide does not solve any problems, and there's bad karma associated with it. Therefore, I will subject this body to environmental toxins until it quits working on its own.

The alternative interpretation says, "I am not aware enough of who I really am to stay and function in this world. My lack of awareness is making me make bad choices that lead to unnecessary experiences, and I am getting more bound here rather than freer. Unless I take the right steps to expand my awareness to include my Divinity, I might as well cash in this body and get another one later and try again to learn these lessons."

The question always remains: Do I drop the body now, or do I have more service to do here that requires a body? I have a plan for more service that requires the body (writing and other stuff), so for now, my choice is to keep it well and functioning. That also gives me more time with my saint of a wife, Carol, who is the love of my life.

> If we accept restriction, we manifest restriction. It's true on the physical level, also. If you feel you are not worthy of a great job, a particular salary, or a loving spouse, you create your own restriction. When you believe you are worthy of good things, good things come to you. Believing in yourself is a way you receive and use Spirit's Light energy.
>
> On the spiritual levels, too, I experienced that as long as I could keep expanding and supporting my value to receive more of God's Light and Sound, I could keep moving up in these spiritual dimensions. If I became judgmental of myself or my process, I shut the process down and could no longer move my awareness to the higher spiritual realms.
>
> —John-Roger with Pauli Sanderson,
> *When Are You Coming Home? A Personal Guide to Soul Transcendence*

—Esther responds to Ken's blog—

I love that you're writing this blog, Ken. There's so much valuable info in your experience that the rest of us could use in one way or another. When we've talked in the past, I often thought you were an excellent communicator of both information and enthusiasm. (You shoulda been a teacher. Well, maybe you are now.) I felt that especially when you talked about Tom Brown's tracker school and your experiences there. I just "got" that perhaps you're on a tracker experience now—an inner-self and body-tracking experience. Interesting metaphor. Thanks for doing this.

—John Lee—

Hi, Ken. Thank you for sharing your insights about the death wish. It helps clarify my own issues. I have been in Thailand for almost three months. I think it is allowing me some respite from my life in LA that has been difficult. You are in my thoughts (and dreams). I love you, John.

Chapter 7

Baja Nutri-Care Clinic

Ken, February 10, 2010

I first went to BNC (Baja Nutri-Care) in July 2009. I was there for three weeks with my sweet, loving wife, Carol. The clinic staff were very caring people and did a great job of taking care of all our needs.

Baja Nutri Care Clinic staff say
goodbye to Ken and Carol

From Carol to my coworkers,

I have been waiting to write this e-mail until I had all my thoughts together, but now I see I need to do it now. Ken is having to stay here at the clinic another week beyond the two we planned because of the spread of the cancer—something we didn't know until we met with the doctors here at the clinic. He is getting extra care like laetrile, vitamin C, extra pancreas nutrition, extra a lot of things to bring on the healing reactions. So at this point he would not be home until December 1. This is a very critical time—they are doing their best to turn it around. And he is experiencing so much benefit from my being with him, doing prayer communion, helping him bathe, and getting him things pretty regularly throughout the day—he has to eat little bits many times a day, and I am hesitant to leave him here for days without me. He is processing so much history, and many sensations in his body are bringing up memories. It helps him so much to have an ear to listen to what he is going through and help him clear it. He's responding so openly to the loving and being touched physically. It's an extraordinary time of healing and blessing—for which I have no adequate words. The Divine energy of Spirit is palpable.

Ken to his sisters,

My personal therapy includes visualizing my body clean, clear, and whole, and filled with Divine Light and awareness several times a day. Carol and I have had some wonderful talks these past days. I can hear and smell the high tide surf as I write this, so life is good.

God bless us all,
Kenny

—A Prayer offered by our dear friend Gail Honeycutt—

Hi there, Joneses,

May the magnificent Light of the Christ, the Traveler, the Holy Spirit, and the collective radiance of all the ministers, rabbis, priests, avatars, yogis, holy beings, students of Light, the angelic host, and all the aspects of God on all the levels of creation, be a joyous, harmonious blend as your support team into full healing in all ways for the Highest Good of both Carol and Ken.

May your consciousnesses align with the Song—the Sound and Frequency of the universes, of creation— that Harmony which brings peace, well-being, health, loving grace, and joyfulness in abundance. May the Song become a balancing connection to your highest goods.

May your souls sing with the Song and know the gifts, the blessings, that this sort of courage brings. And may those gifts and blessings radiate through all your levels of consciousness, loving yourselves into—LIFE.

We are with you, so many of us are with you. Be courageous. Dare to embrace yourselves fully. We love you and offer you this loving.

Gratitude and blessing to you this Thanksgiving season, dear friends.

Love, Gail

—From our sweet cousin, Annabelle—

Kenny, you look even more handsome, if that's possible. I love you with all my heart. Keep following your treatment, and I know you will get better and I can't wait until I can hug and kiss you again. I'm so grateful that Carol picked such a sweet loving, caring, and special guy, and I'm so glad you are part of our family. You and Carol are very precious to me, and I will be praying hard for you both.

Annabelle

Carol wrote to John Morton

Dear John,

Kenny and I thank you so very much for the goodness you bring into our lives. For your personal attention to each one of us and your amazing ability to envision what can be and go toward that, with all of us following in your footsteps. Our days are very tender and sweet and scary at the same time. I am, as you suggested in your last communication to me, intent on turning fear into love, and in that love finding the peace and glory of God.

God bless you John. I love you deeply,

Carol

Chapter 8

The Edge

Ken, February 11, 2010

The Edge of Life and Death

Each day now as I watch more of my physical body disappear to the consumption of melanoma, the edge comes closer, clearer. The relentless progress of the disease is observable in many ways, both in my skin and in my internal body functions.

I have several protruding lesions under my skin that would have raised alarming concerns six months ago, but now are no more than curiosities. However, they give me external markers of the progression of melanoma by how much they protrude, the size, and the color.

The internal symptom that's most responsible for my attention is the bleeding ulcer in my duodenum. I have to be careful of what I eat to avoid aggravating this condition.

I have been losing the layer of lubricating fat between my skin and muscles, so the skin on my feet, calves, ankles, hands, elbows, and knees is like a dried-out sponge. It soaks up aloe vera and flax seed oil like one too.

My physical body is host to a process that is consuming itself. It reminds me of the vacuum-tailed creature in *Yellow Submarine* that sucked itself up into nothing. Why do I do this to myself? Looking at it as a neutral observer, I'd say this body is no longer needed on the planet and is simply going through a natural recycling program instituted by its own internal software that automatically kicks in at a certain point of failure of other meta-programs that were installed at the planning session of the individual with the Karmic Board before this incarnation began.

The efforts of the individual at this point to save the emaciated body and continue using it for service of the consciousness is a questionable goal. However, upon request of the individual, God's grace for that purpose is being extended so a demonstration period can be established and observed for appropriate manifestation.

The failed meta-programs that the Karmic Board put in place were aimed at providing the individual with the appropriate opportunities for learning and growth and furthering the experience of the indwelling soul.

The individual basically made bad choices, indulging instead in the pleasures of the world and letting the learning opportunities pass him by. After tens of thousands of opportunities had been ignored, the board voted to pull the plug on this body and make space on the planet for another soul to seek its experiences and lessons.

The indwelling soul in this body realized what was happening and requested another chance, additional time in this body to be of service and to advance its own enlightenment and liberation from the bonds of the world. And to spend more quality time with his sweetie wife.

The request was granted on a provisional basis, and an agreement was reached. The soul must demonstrate an ongoing commitment to

1. being of service to others
2. using every experience he can for his advancement, learning, and growth toward liberation of the soul
3. taking good care of his sweetie wife.

How the individual carries out the provisions of the agreement will be made on the basis of his individual choices. The karmic board will be observing and evaluating each choice. Latitude will be permitted for the learning process. The board gently reminds the person to have fun, too.

Chapter 9

Calming the Basic Self

Ken, Friday, February 12, 2010

Okay, I'm back.

I have been afraid to go to sleep for fear that I would not wake up again. Turns out, it is my Basic Self that is afraid of being abandoned. He needed comforting and I gave it to him—a caressing, soothing assurance that separating from the body is a natural process, and nothing to worry about. He will go back to where basic selves come from. Michael Hayes said an angel had been placed with my basic self to calm his worries. Perhaps I can now sleep easy and in peace.

I had a PET scan two days ago. If you're not familiar with PET scans, they are graphic pictures of the amount of metabolic activity in the body, specifically the melanoma's growth and spread.

We met with the Burzynski clinic radiologist today to see the scans. We went through the whole body. It was lit up like the Christmas tree at Rockefeller Center, and I mean Broadway marquee level. After taking us through it, he said it was "maximum involvement of melanoma," every kind of tissue, the most he had ever seen in a living human being. After taking a moment to take that in, I said, "Maybe I'll set a new record for recovery."

I asked him if he thought I could still recover, and he said, "I don't know." The doctor assigned to my case said the same and added, "We are doing all we can." She said Dr. Burzynski is working on my case.

Admittedly, the last two days have felt like my body was being consumed by the melanoma so fast it was disappearing into a black hole. Everything was difficult. My skin on my ankles felt like I had extreme sunburn. My arm and leg skin was as wrinkled as a hundred-year-old man's. There was an ominous dark glow all under my chest skin. I was extremely weak. I gave myself less than a week to live.

Yet Friday morning dawned with my feet and ankles showing tendons, meaning the swelling had gone down. I stood with renewed vigor and strength. The skin on my arms and legs was filled out again, wrinkles almost gone. I have to credit the change in diet that includes animal protein as the main cause of my turnaround. Quite literally, I was starving myself to death on my previous diet. Well, the new diet of eat anything and everything has made a big difference. But my digestive system has slowed down to the point that it's hard to get anything to go all the way down.

—Esther—

I love this—the neutrality and clarity of it, the angel's eye view, the humor. Grace, grace, exquisite grace.
Hope to see you soon, Ken.

—Ginny Fraser—

Ken, I am so in awe of your wisdom and the humor and Light that comes through your blog. I think what you're writing is so important for others to read and share as an example of a gigantic soul taking the steps, taking the steps, being present, being present, moving on, moving on with such grace.

Love and much Light to you
Ginny

—Babalola Chris-Rotimi—

Dearest Ken,

You soul brother, you! I am blessed to be sharing in the wisdom of your loving heart through these blog posts. And I am even more blessed to be a part of your (and Carol's) life at this time.

Yes, Ken, I am all for you setting that new record for recovery! From all I have read and heard you share so far, it would seem to me like every single moment you continue to breathe in and out under your present circumstances is a record, for which I join with you in blessing God's Holy name. Peace, be still, bro! And keep on blogging...

Babalola

—Kenny replied—

Hi, Babalola,

Since I did not have any brothers growing up, I was always looking for that playmate who could be like a brother to me. Little did I know one of my true soul brothers was born in Nigeria... my brother from another mother. That was you!

I say soul brother because it means we both know we are divine souls having experiences as human beings. There is no delusion here about the trappings of the world as part of our identity. We are one in Christ, in the Mystical Traveler Consciousness, and the Divine Beloved.

And what great joy and peace and freedom it is to know and be that.

Soul Brother, Babalola, in Kenny's Virgil Cole hat.

—Cousin Doug Cowan—

Dear Ken,

I regret that I had such little opportunity to hang out with you after we cousins sort of scattered to the four winds long ago. Your soft spoken kindness and gentle sense of humor made a lasting impression on me however. I love that we did get together after many years and were able to chill out a bit at the Island house, do some sailing, get caught up, and meet each other's wives. We'll be watching your excellent blog and you are very much in our thoughts. Keep up the great work, and Dori and I hope for the very best for you and your family.

Love, Doug

—Daniel Safron—

Dear Ken,

I just read you blog for the first time and was moved, touched, lifted, blown away. Thank you for your immense loving and profound wisdoms.

I'll share it with friends. God bless you on your journey and it's been a real pleasure knowing you (you too, Carol!). 'Til we meet again.

Love and Light,
Daniel Safron

Chapter 10

The Talk with Melanoma

Ken, February 19, 2010

Last night I had a heart-to-heart talk with my melanoma (M). We created a safe space to share, and I started by reviewing how and why M came to be in my life. There were both conscious and unconscious elements present in that manifestation.

My intention was to establish my position as a neutral observer toward M so there was no intimidation in either of us in giving clear and accurate information.

I spoke from the position of authority and took responsibility for having invited M into my life. The etheric form of M lightly lit on my shoulder one fine day like a butterfly and burrowed into a mole that had been there for years. It was the size of a blink and used an allergy as an entry point. There were two implants, but the second one died.

The mole began to "mogrify" [Ken's word] to accommodate the increased metabolic activity, and M settled in for the long haul. I told M that it had served its purpose and was no longer needed to bring me a message of failed purpose in my life. I got the message and knew that being of service is the way to go.

I told M it can now go back into the nothingness from which it had come.

The Burzynski medications will help it do that with grace and ease.

Chapter 11

New Developments

Ken, February 23, 2010

I had several days of low points and couldn't blog, but now I'm on the mend and am back.

We did a blood draw this morning, and my hemoglobin was back down to a very low 8.7. So early tomorrow morning, we pack a breakfast, a snack, and all my meds and food supplements, and I check into the emergency room at the nearby Memorial Hermann Hospital complaining of shortness of breath and internal bleeding and ask to see a specific doctor, Kuliev, who has arranged an "emergency"' nuclear bleeding scan.

As an outpatient, I get injected with a radioactive isotope that illuminates bleeding spots. I wait a long while, they take a picture of my whole small intestine, and I go home tomorrow afternoon.

Repeat same procedure on Wednesday, except I may not have to be injected with the isotope again; we may go on from there with a procedure.

Either Wednesday or Thursday, Dr. Raza will do an emergency cauterization of all the bleeding spots in my small intestine to stop the internal bleeding. What luck! Dr. Raza is the only doctor in Houston who is qualified to do this procedure. He will go in through a series of arteries to seal the spots rather than with surgery. We ask God for there to be a small number to seal.

Most likely this will be a permanent end to the internal bleeding, because Dr. Burzynski's targeted gene therapy and my working with the Light of God have the melanoma on the retreat.

Pretty exciting, no? These current days bring their own reward that is magnificent beyond compare. You, dear friend, may be familiar with religious writings about oneness with God. When that happens to you, all other considerations fall into line, and staying in the oneness becomes paramount. Also, much more fun.

Carol writes:

> Ken never had the emergency cauterization—his cancer symptoms were too advanced to attempt the procedure. Instead he spent ten days at Memorial Hermann Hospital chasing the symptoms. See chapter 14: Houston Is Probably a Nice Place, for more details.

Chapter 12

Kenny Talks about his Ministry and the Cancer-Healing Affirmation

Ken, March 1, 2010

(From a recording of Kenny talking about his ministry at the Candlewood Inn, Houston Texas, 3:23 a.m.—one of those nights he couldn't sleep.)

My ministry is my calling. And God, I ask at this time to continue this lifetime and manifest that dream and minister to that calling. I need this body to do it with. So let's keep it alive. My ministry and my service is through writing and speaking to bring the message to people of the divinity and the perfection of the soul. And the beauty and the order and the peace that can be brought forward on the planet through the manifestation of soul in all areas of human activity.

It's time to tap into it and do it. That's my message.

Part of my job is to find examples to show what people are doing to manifest the soul on the planet and to manifest it myself. Ministering through whatever they are doing, bringing forward magic on the planet through their awareness of the power of Divine Being. It could be any area of life, any expression of the arts or their work. It could be a sheep rancher, a high school teacher a performing artist. Anybody. All will recognize divine soul principles when they see them. I will write about them and speak about them.

The calling is to celebrate, record, and express the manifestation of the Divine Soul on the planet through any means possible.

Carol said: *You know you are manifesting your soul's purpose right now.*

Kenny said: *Yes I do. I'm manifesting my soul's purpose already, right now to heal this body, so I can carry out these plans.*

March 9, 2010

Cancer-Healing Affirmation

I ask for the Light of the Christ for the highest good for all concerned. I picture myself enveloped in the flames of the Burzynski medications. The flames are burning all the cancer cells, and the heat causes the white blood cells to multiply and come forth like an army.

I send the white blood cell army to all the cancer tumors and visualize them being digested and having their food and blood supply being cut off.

I send the white blood cell army wherever there is cancer. I stop the cancer cells' ability to communicate with one another. I use the white blood cell army to gather up the cancer cells, and dissolve them in the Light of The Christ.

I visualize myself being rained on with blue green healing energy. I next form a grid of white light around myself that seals in the healing energy. Finally, I visualize myself completely healthy for the highest good of all concerned.

Carol writes: *This book is dedicated to manifesting Kenny's ministry as he shared it with me that early morning when he couldn't sleep just twenty-nine days before he passed into Spirit. May it fall into the hands of every person who can benefit from reading about the view of Spirit* Through Kenny's Eyes.

Kenny wrote: I do not know what Spirit has in store for me. I will keep breathing as long as Spirit gives me breath. And if melanoma absolutely must claim my body, it can have it. Melanoma cannot go where I go, because I go into the pure Spirit of the Soul Realm that is my true home.

Chapter 13

Giving Up?

Ken, March 9, 2010

Today I found myself giving up on my chances for recovery from cancer, but for no real reason. My friends had not given up on me, miraculous as it sounds. Yes, we are flying back to Prana tomorrow, but that doesn't mean the Burzynski medications are not going to work for me. I will continue taking what I can of them, and combined with my cancer-healing affirmation, I may be able to heal the cancer. Light on all that for the highest good of all concerned.

I can still walk a bit, and I have a good appetite if I eat what Spirit directs me to eat. I can have bowel movements, even if it means painful Fleet enemas. I still have Carol's undying devotion to do anything and everything to take care of me and make me comfortable. I still have Dr. Burzynski's willingness to work with me and provide the medications that can overcome the cancer. I still have the love and support and faith of friends who are constantly sending me the audible Light Stream of God. And I am still having miracles of perfect timing happening everyday to keep me going.

So there is no reason to give up. I hereby let go of all and any reason to give up on my recovery from cancer and I allow myself any and all chances for a full recovery.

Well, I'm still here. After an amazing travel day from Houston to LA, and a very difficult night back at Prana, I find myself still breathing and carrying on. The night was difficult because Carol and I were both up all night dealing with a series of small bowel movements. A nurse is coming this morning to help us with all that. We are considering getting a hospital bed in here.

—Ben Underwood responds to Ken's blog—

I have just found out that you have cancer. I pray for your recovery and for you to get back your healthy body. We were best friends for many years, and I have not forgotten the great fun we used to have. Your family was my family. I probably spent more time at the Joneses than I did at my own home. Your mom and dad were two of the finest people I have ever known (so were Genia, Karen, Debbie, and Cynt). I still have a warm feeling when I ride by your home-place. You hang in there, old buddy—if anyone can, it will be you—love you old friend—Ben

—Donna Hall Kater—

Hi, Ken and Carol. I am sending you both Light, love, and blessings right now. I am so grateful for our friendship that started many years ago. I am grateful that our lives crossed paths many times over the last twenty-five years or so. Touched, I am. Haven't seen you for a while, but know that my love and friendship for you both is as strong as ever.

I am comforted by the knowledge, Ken, that you know who you are whether you are in a body or not.

Your spirit is shining so brightly right now, even as your body is doing whatever it is doing.

I have worked a lot with hospice, as a counselor, as an acupuncturist, and as a family member of a loved one who has been under hospice care. It is one of the most wonderful things on the planet, and you will be well taken care of. There is a lot of help both for you and for your family members.

You are in my thoughts and prayers every day as you make this journey.

Love, Donna

—Babalola—

Hey, Kenny Boy,

Notice that sweet, sunny smile that just popped up in your heart? That's a picture of my face you carried with you from Houston back to LA.

Know that you are in my heart just as I am in yours and that we are both in the heart of God. Pretty nice place to be, eh?

Your Soul Brother (::)
Babalola

—Kenny replied—

That sweet sunny smile that just popped up in my heart is one of the most precious things in my life right now. I cherish the time we spent together in Houston, getting to know each other and finding each of us to be a true Soul Brother. Being in the heart of God with you is the best. No reason to ever be anywhere else. We will always be together here, sharing in the audible Light Stream of God.

What's that I hear? The ocean surf, or a mountain waterfall? It is so compelling. Maybe it is the wind from the canyon pass like a thousand violins. So sweet.

Light to your trip home and to your loving and beautiful family in Houston. Light to your Mother and family.

I love you, my brother, Kenny Boy

Ken, February 2010

Well of Souls

I look at my future now, and I see that my physical body is very close to dropping into the Well of Souls. There are so many signs of deterioration, degeneration, and decaying of my body that it's a wonder I'm still walking around. I'm pretty sure that my oncologist has seen melanoma take down so many people that he has formed a picture of what it looks like at each step along the way, and has a head movie of the Melanoma Melodrama: from Start to Finish.

As one who never opted for any form of chemo, I can say that my quality of life has steeply increased as my disease has steadily progressed. I feel as though I am among the "Living Free." I have so little standing between me and my awareness of God that practically all I see is beauty. I take meds to control the pain, and I handle the basic body functions to keep it going, and my consciousness dances free in the Light of God.

Chapter 14

Houston Is Probably a Nice Place

Carol remembers the February 2010 trip to Houston that Kenny talked about in Calming the Basic Self (see chapter 9).

I look back on that month in Houston where Kenny sought treatment for his cancer, and it appears dark, scary, and full of anxiety—yet at the same time filled with the miracles of perfect timing and spiritual assistance. Overall, though, I would have liked to skip the day-to-day-ness and just learned the lessons. It was the toughest four weeks of my life, with Kenny very obviously losing one body function after another daily. So while Houston is probably a nice place, not so much in my memory.

When we left the Gerson clinic in Tijuana at the end of November 2009, because the melanoma had infiltrated Kenny's brain, it was recommended that we look into the Burzynski clinic in Houston. They are known for working with cancers in the brain. We applied, submitting some sixty pages, including all his lab reports since the original mole was diagnosed as melanoma in 2000. He was accepted for a start date of February 9, 2010. We took all the steps to prepare for the trip—this last-ditch effort to halt the onslaught of the monster invading his body. It was going to be two weeks of outpatient care with overnight accommodations at a nearby hotel, and then back home to LA for follow-up treatment.

The day before we left, one of our dear friends, who is a runner, showed us the DVD of a 5K run she had dedicated just that weekend to Kenny's recovery. It was a sweet moment of prayer and communion. By this time Kenny had lost about forty pounds, was looking very thin, and felt weak compared to his old self. They had found a lesion in his digestive tract that was bleeding, and he already had several blood transfusions. He needed assistance showering and drying off; he was slow and deliberate in his movements and not able to drive. Another longtime friend offered to assist Kenny with showers in the mornings, and that was such a treat for all of us. You see, I had been showering Kenny myself for several weeks, and it was one of the most precious moments of the day. An honoring of his body, a blessing, a sweet and profound time of caretaking. Kenny loved it and I loved it. And when we asked Kevin to assist so I could prepare breakfast at the same time, he loved it too.

Back to Houston. The Heartfelt Organization and Thelene Scarborough, a minister in MSIA who lived in Dallas, had enlisted the assistance of ministers in Houston to help when we arrived. Jesus Ordonez bought all our groceries. Yvette was to learn to make juices for us and clean the kitchen in our suite almost daily. Joaquin came to visit about three times a week to chat and hold the Light. When Kenny's Soul Brother, Baba, arrived a week later, he visited every single day and did errands as needed, spent the night so I could rest, and arranged a ministers' meeting right in our hotel suite. Jesus did the laundry, made the bed, and helped Kenny shower many times during our stay. Our little army of soldiers was on the march with whatever was needed.

The second day at the clinic, Ken was scheduled for a scan to assess the extent of the melanoma. He wasn't allowed to eat or drink anything until after the procedure, which was late due to another patient's emergency. I was frantic with worry because he had been getting dehydrated very easily. One of the most precious services MSIA ministers perform is prayer. I called home (MSIA headquarters) and asked that an all-call go out to everyone in the building to pray—to send the spiritual Light of healing to Kenny and to the procedure immediately. Often we don't know how God responds to our prayers, but this time I was sure the Light of God was comforting me, while forever-optimistic Kenny was certain everything would be okay all along. I prayed for Divine intervention and finally the procedure was underway—four hours after we were supposed to go back to the hotel. Finally he could eat a meal and drink his precious carrot-apple juice—we were still following the Gerson protocol. That was Wednesday. Thursday we saw the nutritionist, who immediately put Kenny on a protein-rich diet—his blood work showed advanced anemia, and he was very weak. It was time to "beef" up his intake after five months of a completely vegan diet, part of the Gerson plan. This was another blow to the belief that Kenny could reverse the melanoma march.

Friday we had an appointment to view the scan with the doctor and the radiologist. Both were stunned at what they saw. Kenny's entire torso was blackened on the silhouette drawing; on the scan pictures, tumors lit up like lightbulbs everywhere, most of them concentrated in his torso, but scattered throughout his limbs, neck, and head as well. We heard the radiologist saying, "I've never seen so much involvement in any other patient." They would try to help, they said. Kenny replied, "Maybe I'll be your Burzynski poster child." But we walked out of the clinic that day heavy with the reality of what we had seen.

The next week presented the inevitable complication: Kenny needed another transfusion. It was off to the First Street Hospital to be admitted to their emergency room to wait for blood to arrive. It took all day for blood to show up. In the meantime, our own crew of ministers came to us with food and juice, and sweet Grace drove all the way from Austin with delicious homemade soup and bread. How tenderly we were ministered to, how dearly these people who hardly knew us were caring for us. I was in tears most of every day, either from gratitude or from worry or from venting anxiety or sadness or resignation, or lack of sleep or... Kenny was too, but mostly from gratitude.

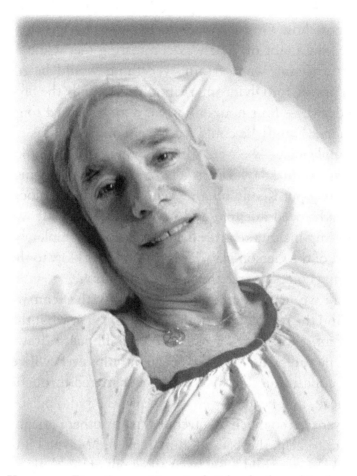

Kenny at First Street Hospital. I looked at this dear photo on my phone, and as much as I denied it, I began to sense these would be his last days.

Finally, the next day, all the blood was in Kenny's veins, and he was released to go back to the hotel. Some more visits to the clinic in the next few days, some more good food, juices, clinic-prescribed drugs (some of which were a type of medications that presented their own set of really uncomfortable symptoms), and it was back to the hospital again for the next blood transfusion.

Only this time he was to be admitted as an inpatient for ten days to handle one advanced melanoma symptom after another. Clinic drugs were suspended while IVs and blood were administered along with his anti-brain swelling medicine, his thyroid medicine, and a host of other pills. In his later blogs, he talks about how precious it was to have a bowel movement. It became tougher and tougher, and one remedy after another was suggested. None worked very well, and the daily battle to complete the cycle of eating and eliminating dragged on. After months of urinating a surprising couple of gallons each day, even urinating became a problem until the Foley catheter was inserted, bringing blessed relief. All the while, I slept in the visitor chair in the hospital room night after night, going back to the hotel every couple of days only to shower while one of our dear friends stayed with Kenny. I made sure he was never alone, never without an MSIA minister or initiate by his side.

It was time to transfer Kenny from the ICU floor to a regular room in another wing. The internist visited to draw up the release papers. He suggested Kenny might want to think about getting home as soon as we could and arranging for hospice care. Kenny declined and said he would resume his Burzynski therapy. The doctor and nurse took me aside outside the room and with saddened urgency said we had only a short window of time to go home before he could not travel on conventional flights. Eventually he would need a special medically equipped charter flight that would be cost-prohibitive. I couldn't believe what I was hearing. I was seeing it with my own eyes, yet I couldn't fully grasp that Kenny was slipping away at such a fast rate now. Every day another body function was compromised.

Just a day later, the gastroenterologist blustered in after we were settled in the new room. "Do you know about a bucket list? Well, it's time to make yours," he announced. "Eat anything you want and do whatever you want. Okay, buddy?"

Did all our mouths drop open? Did we hear him right? Who trained him in his delicate bedside manner? I was livid with disbelief. Couldn't say a word, and neither could Kenny or Baba. We just let him disappear out of the room as if he had never showed up. Kenny was bent on continuing his Burzynski therapy.

Sometime between hospital visits in Houston, though, Kenny said to me, "Carol, I don't think I'm going to make it." I knelt beside his chair and began to sob. I said to him, "Oh, Kenny, don't say that. You're still in treatment, and don't we believe it will work?" His response was something like, "Okay, yes, we're still in treatment."

Now it seems apparent to me that what he really meant was, "Okay, Carol, I know you can't handle it, so I won't talk about it anymore. But the reality is I'm dying." Just about a month earlier I had heard him talking to a friend about a favor he was asking someone to do for him and the phrase "You wouldn't refuse a dying man, would you?" flew through the air and stuck in my skull like a speeding bullet. But just like all the other signals that he was declining rapidly now, I stuffed that one in an airtight compartment in the far reaches of my consciousness. Denial—that my strong, tall, handsome, smart, funny, and beautiful husband was slipping into the Well of Souls.

But I did listen to Doc #1 and suggested to Kenny that we do what we could to get home while he could still get on a plane and off again. He was walking very little now, had to be hoisted out of his chair and tucked into bed at night, but we knew what we had to do. Making arrangements to go home was in itself a relief. The timing of every occurrence in Houston was perfect. We prayed Spirit would meet us at the point of our action and it did, time and time again. We asked and prayed fervently that Spirit would fill in the gaps when we didn't know what the next step would be, and it did.

A view into the future.
Photo used with permission from MSIA.

If I had been more present with Kenny, I would have listened to him talk about how he felt about not making it. I would have opened my mind and heart to hear him and hold him while he talked. I would have remembered that when my father died, I had done the same thing. He said, "Carol, it won't be long now." My answer was, "Oh, Daddy, you seem to be getting better, aren't you?" He shrugged his shoulders and raised his eyebrows in an expression of doubt and resignation, and passed away three days later.

So while memories of Houston flood up during this one-year anniversary since we embarked on that never-to-be-forgotten journey, I'm here to suggest you come present with your loved ones and talk about the inevitable. One of you will leave this world before the other, and it will be impactful and profound—and oh so worth sharing about from the sincerity and tenderness of the Spiritual Heart.

Words of wisdom from the Spiritual Heart come from many people and experiences in our lives. My long-time friend and director of the Heartfelt Foundation, Patti Rayner, shared one of the most important wisdoms at such a profound time in Kenny's and my life.

—Esther—

I'm right there with you, Carol. Visualizing Kenny, the hospital bed, the hotel, the group of ministers who so loved to participate with you and Ken. Please be very gentle with yourself as you relive these events. Love, E

—Sandra Dupont—

Oh Carol, I am so moved by your sharing… I think it is precious and courageous of you to revisit these memories, as well as share them with us.

I agree that it is essential to try and be fully present with our loved ones—with what they are going through, and how they are feeling. At the same time, it is entirely understandable that the challenge of seeing a loved one in pain could cause us to turn away from the reality of the situation.

Your writing is so tender and transparent that I find myself transported through time, walking beside you and Kenny in your journey, loving you both.

From Patti Rayner, Executive Director, Heartfelt Foundation
HeartReach and Circle of Light
March 4, 2010

Dearest Carol,

You're doing such a great job ... with everything.

My heart's urging for you now is to see if you can move into less doing and more being with Ken and spending precious, easy moments with him. I know how sweet your relationship has become, and I'm so happy you have more help with the doing right now.

So, since we don't know what Kenny's soul has chosen as his highest good, you may want to ask yourself, What are the things I'd want to say or do if his soul had made the choice for him to leave? You may find that everything has been said and done. You may find that there are a few things that haven't. If so, do those, just to open up the space for an even deeper level of communication for you both.

It seems clear that one of the things chosen for him is that you two be there for now. I'm so grateful that you have a little family support team around you in such a deep and blessed way. God is so amazing and His ways are wondrous!

All of your family here walk through this with you both, hold for you, love you, and are here to assist in any way, Carol. And of course, your greater global family send enormous Light. I'm so appreciative to be kept in the loop and receive your updates. I'm here twenty-four/seven, as you know.

With love and blessings, Patti

Carol added: God bless us all, and may we embrace each experience as an opportunity to love and forgive and learn and come present.

—Denise Lumiere—

Carol, you are such a writer and what a story! There is
so much here! In the depth of what you went through,
there is something that transcends and teaches. I can't
put it into words but am deeply grateful and appreciate
so much what you are doing with this. I hope this is a
book in process as it is just amazing.
    Love,
    Denise

Chapter 15

The Plane Ride Home from Houston, March 9, 2010

Carol remembers...

We had taken the doctor's advice to leave Houston for home as soon as possible while Kenny could still fly on a commercial plane. He was extremely weak, mustering up all the strength he had each day to walk from the bed to the chair, get dressed, bathe, have meals, and a visit to the clinic here and there. And of course he needed help with all of that. By this time, his entire body was riddled with melanoma; I could feel the lumps in his stick-thin arms and even see a crusty one just behind his left ear. His blood supply was dangerously low and waning every day. But my husband had the strength and endurance of a race horse, the determination of a man with a mission, and the acceptance of an ascended master. As this story progresses, you'll see for yourself how these attributes supported his final trip home to our beloved Prana.

That Saturday, Baba arranged to have a recorded MSIA seminar right in our hotel suite. Marsha and Rosie drove all the way from Austin to be with us. They stayed the night. Thelene drove five hours from Fort Worth. And Juaquin and Yvette made it too. There we were, eight of us calling ourselves forward into the Light, sharing the depth of our prayers and our gratitude, and just simply being there in support of one soul's journey into the arms of God. My prayer was not only for Kenny's healing but for a safe and easy trip home.

On Sunday, Rosie and Marsha bought us a bunch of groceries, including a good, old-fashioned, head-kickin' Texas barbeque lunch, which Kenny devoured with glee. And since that rude and crude bucket-list doctor told him he could eat and drink whatever he wanted (after all, without saying, he really meant, "These are your last days, buddy"), Kenny promptly ordered Baba to bring in some really good booze. I can't remember what it was, but it didn't go unnoticed.

On Monday, I didn't know how I was going to get Kenny on and off the plane. He was using a walker now and could only manage a few steps. I was consumed with grief and worry. I didn't know how it could be done. I felt helpless. While Kenny was napping in the bedroom, I silently cried my eyes out on the couch in the living room as I made arrangements on the phone for a flight home the next day. But I also prayed. I remembered how Spirit had met us at the point of each action and filled in the gaps wherever necessary time and time again during that month in Houston. In fleeting moments of awareness, I put my trust in God, that the Omniscient and Divine would pave the way, that our trip home would be graceful and easy—through all our circumstances.

It was Tuesday now, the day we would fly. I began to pack, and the lovely woman we hired to help care for Kenny while we were in Houston emptied the entire refrigerator and the cupboards of our personal food supplies. Juaquin packed all the stuff he agreed to ship home for us, like the juicer and the strainer and the immersion blender, and I crammed everything I could into our luggage including the new Tony Lama boots, and the books, and the medications, and the everything, oh and Valentine Tiger.

Carol, Kenny, and Valentine Tiger

Thankfully, Baba followed me to the car rental drop-off, which was only blocks from the hotel, and then he drove us straight to the airport in his car. Two porters were waiting for us, one with a wheelchair for Kenny and the other to help me with our carry-ons. They escorted us all the way to the gate and stayed with us until we were called to board.

I can't express how dear and exciting and relieving it was to be coming home after the harrowing month in Houston, which included Kenny's painful reaction to the new medications, the overwhelming and dreaded results of the CT scan, the blood transfusions, the hospital stays; and the masked knowing underlying all the busyness of each day was that the Well of Souls would be calling Kenny's name soon, signaling the end as we knew it, and the beginning of his journey home to the Heart of God.

He was wheeled right up to the door of the plane. In his shearling slippers (the only shoes that would fit his swollen feet), we slowly shuffled together to our seats at the bulkhead. There was me walking backward holding Kenny's hands to help keep him steady and attendants standing by helpless because the aisle would only accommodate us two. Finally we reached our seats, Kenny as handsome as ever in his Virgil Cole cowboy hat and me in my Boss of the Town 100 percent beaver fur hat that Kenny had commissioned especially for us by a world-renowned cowboy hat maker in Canada. They were mighty fine hats indeed.

Kenny and Carol with Kenny's Virgil Cole Beaver Fur hat

Such are the blessings. The flight attendants did their best to be helpful. And so did many of the other passengers. The flight was short (whew!) and it was time to land—I say that with gratitude that Kenny's feet could soon be elevated to relieve the swelling. As usual, the captain's voice boomed through the cabin announcing our upcoming landing. Only this time, he told us we were being met by some gusty winds that would buffet the plane around a bit. Kenny held my hand as he always sensed my nervousness on take-offs and landings. And yes, siree, as we descended, the plane bounced and bobbed, swaying to and fro, and I could hear Kenny asking for the Light of the Holy Spirit to be with us and especially with the captain and the ascended masters as well. In fact, it was time for all the masters that work with us to line up in support of a smooth landing.

We touched down one wheel at a time and breathed a sigh of relief. Kenny was in tears of recognition and gratitude. Even now in his weakened state when it would take all his strength, fortitude, and focus to get from his seat in the plane to the wheelchair awaiting us in the jetway, he called forth the Holy Spirit and the entire MSIA ministerial body to assist in the landing. I was struck once again by Kenny's unwavering focus and determination.

Now it was time to get to that wheelchair in the jetway. The attendants had called ahead to make sure porters would be waiting for us and they were. We were the last to get off the plane. We helped Kenny to his feet and ever so slowly and painstakingly, hands in my hands, he reached the chair. I could see he was focusing on balance. With hardly any strength left in his muscles, he now had to consciously make sure he was balanced from head to toe or else the lack of strength could knock him over. I was in awe of what I was seeing. It was not new to me, his determination. I had seen it before, but never to this extreme. In the background, I heard the attendants remark, "We have a disabled man slowly deboarding the plane. It's going to be very slow."

Dear Ross met us at baggage claim and drove us those fateful miles home. Home was in sight now. We made it home. Today is March 7, 2011, just one year and two days from the real "Coming Home to Prana Day." And just twenty-four days shy of the one year anniversary of Kenny's "Coming Home to God Day."

As I look ahead, there may be one more article as I plan for a gathering of loved ones on March 30, the anniversary of his passing, to remember our Kenny in his vitality and wide-eyed enthusiasm for life. He was especially home in nature, hearing birds calling, being held close to the breast of the forest, watching a racehorse full out in the straightaway. Kenny would be embracing us with his magnetic blue eyes and forever smile.

Later I am seeing an accounting of my personal healing from the trauma of my husband's illness and subsequent death, and the many traumas I experienced throughout this life. The frozen synapses thaw out, the resiliency restores, the freedom of choice and walking the high country is within sight. The Father in heaven holds his hands out to me, kind of like I held my hands out to Kenny, although not for balance, but ready to receive whatever I can let go of, whatever I don't need any longer. The ancient protection of the reptilian mind (good for real physical danger but now outdated for emotional or mental challenges) is assigned its rightful job ready for only when needed instead of being revved up nonstop. The nervous system repairs, and the true protection of being present in the *now* anchors deep in my consciousness.

The rest of our story is in previous articles. I hope you are touched by the Spirit as you read, and that you look into your own consciousness once again for the places that call out to be healed. God bless you, Baruch Bashan—the blessings already are.

———

—Babalola—

Brilliant and heartfelt as always, Carol! Thank you!
As the first-year anniversary of Kenny's departure from this physical realm approaches, know that you

are in our hearts and prayers each and every day... for healing, for clearing, for balancing, and for Spirit-guided closures... always for the highest good of all concerned.

Thank you and Kenny for ministering to us even more than we ministered to you.

The Entire MSIA Houston Ministerial Community

—Heather Brown—

Carol. I am reading more now. I feel Ken's presence too. God bless you. You are an inspiration as always. I appreciate so much what you are doing here. You help me carry on. I feel alone, and you have gone before.

Love and Light, Heather in Toronto

Chapter 16

The Day Kenny Chose Hospice Care

Carol, January 18, 2011

It was March 11, 2010, just two days after arriving back home from our trip to the Burzynski Cancer Clinic in Houston, Texas. Houston was quite another story. But the significance of March 11 is our appointment with the oncologist, who had told us he'd do whatever he could to carry on the medications prescribed at the clinic. By this time, Kenny wasn't walking much. He had a Foley catheter and was on a zillion medications for just as many symptoms.

I wheeled him into the patient room where we waited for the doctor. He came in with his assistant. Kenny had lost a lot of weight and was very weak. When the oncologist saw the actual line-by-line treatment plan, contradictory to the Burzynski Clinic protocol, he announced to us that in all good conscience, he could not administer these drugs for Kenny's condition. We asked what the alternative was, and gingerly he took this opportunity to mention hospice—again. In July '09 we didn't give it a second thought. In December we interviewed the hospice worker just to see what it was all about and refused to start because it meant no more blood transfusions, and we knew we were headed for many more.

But this time, Kenny jumped at the chance to say, "That's what I want." I looked at him incredulously, and my heart sank like a lead weight into my stomach. Choking on a giant knot in my throat, I was speechless, heartbroken, and in shock. Fighting back the sobs I really wanted to let out, all I could say was, "Really, Kenny? Really?" After all these months of focusing every waking moment on Kenny's care, now we were to focus on his dying. This was so not in my plan, though it began to be evident way back in November, that there might be no turning back, that Kenny's body was headed for the "Well of Souls," as he'd coined it. But I had a way of stuffing these day-by-day awarenesses somewhere where I could hide them from myself. If we were deeply involved in treatment plans like the Gerson protocol or the Burzynski Clinic, how could I also embrace that he was dying? I couldn't.

So while I was reeling with this new era of preparing for him to die, I busied myself with all the hospice arrangements there were to be made—the hospital bed, the wheelchair, the oxygen machine, the nurse appointments, the calls from the hospice minister and the social worker. Kenny, on the other hand, was continuing not his valiant battle against cancer, but his journey into the Soul Realm where every day, as he drew nearer to his final day, his peace and love and joy and gratitude brought him to levels of realizing himself as one with God with no obvious boundaries. Every day he expounded another seminar about our precious spiritual teachings. Every day he would tell me what he was grateful for. He said, "I'm a happy man. I have everything I need, plus my loving family and friends and you." Every day I would say something like, "Kenny, you're my hero. My one and only love of my life." He would say back, "Carol, you're the love of my life."

And for a while, while he still had some strength, the way he would get into bed was to put his arms around my neck while I swung him from sitting on the side of the bed to lying down. And that's how we'd get him up in the morning. Precious moments, these embraces. They would be the last times he would hug me, though I could kiss him, hold his hand, and wash him, brush his hair, dress him, and feed him until the very end. These were all precious moments that remain as symbols of the depth of our love. They remind me of the oneness we both experienced in each other. Both of us headed in the same direction, both of us responding to his every need every moment of every day.

One day we were lying close in bed, and he managed to put his hand on my chest. Kenny had big, comforting hands with a healing touch. Even in his last days, he was able to transmit that healing energy to me. I cried like a baby—no, I cried like a wife who was losing her husband. Any day now he could be gone. Any day now the Well of Souls would claim him for the last time.

Where did I put all those images and signals that I was losing him? Stacked up somewhere in my consciousness, overshadowed by requiring myself to take Kenny's direction. After all, this was his life, his dying, and his soul's ascension. A celebration awaited him on the other side. I'll find the right words another time to describe how my consciousness worked with compartmentalizing the power of that experience when it becomes clearer to me.

I'm compelled to share with you as many precious moments in these last days as I can remember because of how tender and memorable they were. Somehow remembering them is comforting. In some ways, like when we first fell in love— coming home after a date floating in the euphoria of going over each moment in my mind's eye many times. There is new meaning now to the sentiment, "I only have my memories now." It's sometimes sad, but it also fills me with the experience of deep and abiding love. How divine that is.

Kenny and I are still learning—he, as a soul after consciously dying to this world, and me, as his devoted partner, making my way through the grief of losing him into the peace and loving that awaits my awareness. Little by little I experience myself lifting my Spirit and lightening up. God bless us all.

—Millicent Traiman—

Beloved Carol:

I started reading several blogs on your wondrous, awe-inspiring experiences. It filled me with such tenderness and gratitude and joy for all the understanding and growth we all share. I understand now when I am in soul consciousness with all the compassion I am equipped with... I thank you for that and your heartfelt descriptions of living unto death itself... which I experience as a mere passing into the Oneness.

God bless, dear beloved one. I am loving and embracing you here and now until we all meet in the Oneness again. I am all ways here for you.

LL, Millicent

—Sandra—

Carol, with tears streaming down my face, I mourn for what you lost. But at the same time, I also celebrate the love you shared with your amazing and wonderful husband!

As you said in another post, we will all say good-bye to our life partner at some point. By reading about the gentle and grace-filled way you said good-bye to Kenny, I am learning... about how it is done.

The way to learn about the Soul is to be open to the possibility that it exists; accept the possibility you are more than your body, your thoughts, or your feelings. You don't have to believe it. You don't have to have faith. Just be open to the possibility that it exists.
—John-Roger, *The Way Out Book*

Chapter 17

Triumph of the Spirit

Ken, March 13, 2010

Let's see. Diagnosed in early June with metastasized melanoma. My liver at that time was 70 percent filled with cancer tumors, and my spleen was even worse. It had spread to lymph nodes, ribs, and pelvis and had invaded enough tissue to really scare me. Of course my oncologist recommended chemotherapy to start immediately.

I brought forward the memory of my mother, who had gone to Sloan-Kettering Hospital in New York to get the best care available. They performed horribly disfiguring surgery on her chin and throat. Followed by burning out her salivary glands with radiation, followed by weeks of nausea and weakness brought on by chemo. I am not convinced that the cancer killed her. I held her in my arms as she took her last morphine-filled breath. I told her how much I loved her, and encouraged her to forgive herself for ever judging herself about the way she raised me, or about the way I turned out. Or for anything else in her life, for that matter. Just total self-forgiveness.

She tried to look at me, got big tears in her eyes, and quit breathing. Carol was the only other one there with us when Mom died. Everyone else had just walked out to take a break, having spent time being there with her and saying their good-byes.

Carol and I had just gotten there from a flight from California, so it was our turn.

We were the lucky ones, to watch her last breath. I also got to see Gacky's (Granddad's) last breath, years before. There is something supremely magical about that moment when the spirit of the person escapes the confines of the body and expands into its next level of education in the next realm. Jesus said, "In my house are many mansions." I have often wondered if He was referring to several levels of spirit that exist beyond the physical level rather than just one that everybody calls heaven. I guess I am about to find out. Anyway, I digress.

Diagnosed in June, scanned in July, October, November, February PET showing complete involvement of melanoma in all body tissues, including heart, aorta, bone marrow, several MRIs showing mets [metastases] in the brain growing, ultrasounds, twelve blood transfusions of multiple pints of blood, pneumonia... I mean, folks, I think I may have set some kind of record for having the most melanoma a living human being can have and still be alive. My radiologist in Houston even said that to me—the most he had ever seen.

So today is Saturday, March 13, 2010. Nine months since my diagnosis. If I were a woman, I could have given birth by now.

Let's count my blessings.

I have no pain to speak of, since my new hospice nurse (Lorraine) has so graciously fixed my previously painful bowel movement problem. I have friends all over the world sending me continuous Light and Love, and friends right here at Prana who can drop by and bless me with the most amazing prayer communion and blessings. I have wonderful food prepared for me daily. I have new equipment in my room to make my life more convenient and simple and comfortable. I have my medications that I need. I got very loving phone calls from my sisters, Cynthia, Debbie, and Eugenia. Last night, I easily walked up and down the hall with my walker. I got to watch *Appaloosa* again last night, for the twelfth time. I have my new all-beaver fur Virgil Cole hat with a horse tail twist hat band and a red-tailed hawk feather in it.

And to top it all off, I have the most loving, devoted, sweet, caring, serving, responsible, coordinating, cute, affectionate, sexy, huggable, saint of a wife anyone could possibly imagine in Carol. If MSIA granted annual sainthood awards, she would be the first I would nominate. You would have to have seen her in action to believe the extraordinary level of care she has provided me throughout these last nine months. My best friend, my one and only lover, my partner, my sweet baby.

My soul brother, Babalola Chris-Rotimi, calls me every day to celebrate my triumph of the soul while still in the body.

There can be no other explanation as to why I am still here with a clear consciousness, a positive and cheerful focus, fun-filled and adventurous days, miracles of perfect timing clicking off right on schedule, the continuous spiritual presence of the Mystical Traveler and Jesus Christ, among a large host of other spiritual beings who are enjoying my jokes and wise-cracking. I'm listening closely for the sound current and looking forward to hearing it better.

To what can I attribute all this good fortune? I did it by asking God to grant me some extra time to be of service to anyone I can, in any way I can. I asked that it be done through grace and ease, with the blessings of Jesus Christ.

I think it would be clear to anyone reading this blog that my request had been granted big time.

Sunday, March 21, 2010, just ten days before Kenny left his body, John Morton, spiritual director of MSIA. and his wife, Leigh Taylor-Young Morton, visit Kenny at Prana.

JOHN MORTON: You could be in an upward flow immediately like a Dali Lama who was born under that influence of Spirit—born enlightened in high consciousness—born close. Infants are also close before the veil comes over them—Spirit's close in Spirit. So then as your body is giving you signals like, "Hey, I'm done," go to that place where you are close to Spirit inside and keep it open to whatever God can do—God's miracles and possibilities. That's always wise because something can come as a gift, as an action of Grace.

You can ask, "Why am I still here? The window was open. Because Spirit invited me to do something else." Spirit's plan. Not my life plan. Spirit trumps somebody's destiny. Someone like Jesus is born under that in an amazing way. His whole life was about Spirit's plan. One of the signs is the presence of joy and inspiration.

I've been watching how people are being influenced by your joy. The way you're expressing it as a ministry. They're saying, "God, listen to this?" That's what I'm talking about. What you're doing is the same thing you've always been doing—taking care of yourself. I have that role and you have that role. It's really common sense—ordinary and obvious things.

You can go out searching for something radical. I think you guys did that. Then I have to ask, "Are you enjoying yourself?" Are you on the right track, searching out the next regimen, chasing down the next treatment? What's that doing for you other than you're chasing something you never really get a hold of. You have a responsibility to be in the joy and the upliftment. If someone's missing that, it's unfortunate. But often the karma is so powerful and heavy indicating they are still clearing. This might be called a difficult transition. Sometimes you can't do anything about it. That's how the karma is going to do it.

Obviously I see you being very buoyant, joyful, light, and free. And that's a definite ministry to people. A lot of people don't have that about themselves. They don't want to talk about their transition. They are struggling with it and fighting it, keeping it away as long as possible. But why are they resisting what their life is calling them to do? It's not like giving up. It's cooperating. It's clear to me you're having a lot of fun.

In some ways, I would ask, "What took you so long?" But it doesn't matter because you can't do anything about that. It was the price of admission. You might say, "I had to check this out and check that out and come around to myself and have a much clearer and connected sense of myself. We did the best we could with what we were working with."

I don't sense a struggle with you. I don't think there's a lot of energy in a struggle.

KENNY: Trying to have a bowel movement is a bit of a struggle!

JOHN: That's the ordinariness. What do you do? Soften and tenderize. Don't put something in that's difficult. If the tissues are broken down and they are asking, "Why do you keep sending me stuff?" put yourself in the position of the tissues. Put yourself in a place of compassion at the cell level. How do we do it when I'm still processing and having to eliminate? Have those kinds of talks with yourself. Or have someone who is gifted with this kind of communication help you.

KENNY: It takes a lot of basic self-talk to bring it forward, in a very gentle way, no strain, no pressure. That kind of nurturing talk eventually works.

JOHN: Something you can do is virtual imaging. Go into the creative imagination field. You can do it in other ways also like finding a magazine or a film in which people are moving. Tracking like you love to do or being on a treadmill work also. Get good at passing the message, as clear as waking from a dream where a bear was chasing you so the body connects to the virtual experience. Or it can be as simple as doing what you do when you go for a walk. So the body connects to virtual movement like when you might have taken a constitutional walk. The body is designed to move, not to be stagnant. The tissues are saying, "We are not in a position to do that anymore. Stop."

You might say you can't stop because you still have to process, so have a powwow with yourself, Say, "Okay guys, how would we solve this?"

You wouldn't want to do something that retains water unless it's on purpose, like when there is an injury, for instance. Literally the tissues will swell up so you can't move that body part. So mostly I see remedies that have been known a long time. Hopefully any medication is prescribed by a gifted practitioner and you're taking it like a medicine man would, making it even better. You have that kind of knowledge.

I see a lot of fun around you, joy and peace.

KENNY: See my tiger!

LEIGH: Adorable!

KENNY: My sister sent me this photo album of my life from end to end.

JOHN: I have some photos like this. I was wearing a bow tie. Is this the 1950s?

KENNY: Yes. Thank you for sharing all that with me. I received some stuff I can use like virtual imaging!

JOHN: It's attunement—a great time to be highly attuned and integrated. It's somewhat of a balancing act. How do I do it all? Maximizing levity, buoyancy, clarity, fun and still tending to yourself physically. Your life is obviously significantly different than it was two years ago. But it's not out of balance. In many ways it's more balanced, more rich and fulfilling.

KENNY: Absolutely!

JOHN: Your ministry is on fire.

KENNY: If people could discover the joy I'm having now, they'd stop whatever they are doing and start doing what I'm doing.

JOHN: Let's take a moment now with your permission.

KENNY: Absolutely.

JOHN: Lord God, Jesus Christ, and the Traveler, John-Roger, and all those who gather in this line of the Traveler, and are here spiritually, we are open especially for Ken and for Carol and anybody in this balancing field.

We bring forward all the gifts that are in any way healing and clearing. And once again we go into the line of existence, to the moment of incarnation and this moment, all things are brought together in the perfect pattern of integration.

Find the grace, the beauty, the majesty. We could see it soaring. All things are in this perfect state of movement that we know is the Spirit in all things. Each breath becomes confirmation and also becomes a gift radiating healing. So we see eternally what's going on in all ways. And if there is a letting go and full trust and knowledge that the way is prepared to the very smallest way to the very greatest, we accept and we give thanks and also open up to even greater blessings.

Baruch Bashan (the blessings already are).

KENNY: Thank you, Father; I accept.

JOHN: Okay, my friend, God bless you.

KENNY: Thank you so much. It's been my extraordinary pleasure to have you both here to share today. It's been such a treat. I'm so glad we did it. Hugs all around. Thank you.

John and Leigh in our Boss of
the Town and Virgil Cole hats

Our End-of-Life Spiritual Advisor

Dear Kenny and Carol,

I went to my first lecture by Elisabeth Kübler-Ross, which was life-changing for me, in 1975. I began companioning friends living with life-threatening illness in 1976. I have been very blessed to read your blog yesterday and today.

I wanted to write you to affirm your wisdom and good humor and sureness of life in the spirit. I also wanted you to know that all the love that you share with your loved ones will only increase, though they may not be able to see you in the form they are used to seeing you.

You have everything you need. Your words are a testament to that. The only thing I would suggest is that you and Carol (or anyone else who will) agree on some touchstone symbol of connection (a particular bird, butterfly, etc.) that you can send them when you are in your next cycle. This may sound crazy and may or may not be compatible with your beliefs. Most families were certain I was crazy when I suggested this, but then they would call me and say: "You're not going to believe what just happened!" We would laugh together about the wonderful gift of "coincidence," of timing or electrical "impossibility" that had just occurred... or the cardinal that wouldn't fly away, though only two to three feet away... the butterfly that landed on some loved one's nose!

So I offer this to you in the hopes that the ongoingness of life somehow fits into your life view. It is not intended to diminish any part of your full spiritual potential... it is just a love tap from the other side that brings comfort to those of us left on this side. You write beautifully, and I imagine that your writing will continue in some special way. Clearly you have written beautifully on the hearts of your sisters. You have Karen, your mom and dad, Granma and Gacky waiting for you with open arms whenever you are ready to graduate this part of your journey. I send you thanks for reminding me what I sometimes forget, which you obviously have known all along: "Have fun with your life!" Back atcha. Well done, Kenny. Your birthing will be glorious.

—Kenny replied to our End-of-Life Spiritual Advisor—

What a wonderful idea to choose a touchstone to share with Carol. I have chosen the red-tailed hawk. There is one that lives in our neighborhood that I have seen several times.

A friend of mine recently was standing outside and a tail feather from a red-tailed hawk came floating down from the sky and landed right in front of her. She looked up to see the hawk it came from. She brought me the feather as a gift, and it now resides in my hat band. I will try to send you a photo.

God bless you.
Love and Light,
Kenny Jones

—Teresa Rodgers writes to Ken—

Good morning, Ken,

My heart is so full of loving as I read your post. Your journey is an amazingly blessed one. What courage to truly be who you are in each and every moment and what a gift for us. May you be filled with the Divine Light and may a wave of great peace wash over you with each and every breath. Heartfelt blessing and hugs to you and Carol. God bless you, my friend.

—Susan Tabin—

Dear Ken and Carol,

There are many in your MSIA family residing in the outer bands of LA (Florida for us) who have been sending Light for the highest good and loving you both from the distance.

In certain aboriginal tribes, when a baby is born, the tribe gathers around the newborn baby and says, "We love you and we support you on your journey." When a tribal member is passing, the tribe gathers around and says, 'We love you and we support you on your journey."

And so Ron and I are gathered with you, Ken, to say that we love you and we support you on your journey.

Your sharing is both enlightened and very helpful. Thank you and God bless you both.

Love, Susan and Ron

—Louise Pacheco—

Dear Ken,

Yesterday I received an e-mail from Berti Klein about your situation. It just got me thinking, remembering you and when we first met in San Diego. You were assisting at my Insight Training, standing in the back with the other assistants. I didn't know you then but was struck by the Light I saw in your eyes, and told you so. You were surprised and said, "Thanks."

You were always someone I experienced as quiet and filled with peace, sweetness and loving—and the Light was, is, always in your eyes. It's how I've known and experienced you. Thanks for this blog, and God bless you, Ken.

Lots of LL, Louise

—Joan Shea—

I was delighted to find out about this blog yesterday. What an inspiration you and Carol are! I am touched by your journey and love the way you are demonstrating the more-ness of who you truly are. Light ahead for the highest good. Much loving and peace, Joan

—Denise—

Dear Ken,
Your blog and writings are so sweet and I love both of you. You continue to bring upliftment and gratefulness to the process and yes, you are of service to all of us.
Thank you, dear one!

—Shelley Noble—

Another gorgeous message, Ken. I am deeply honored to witness your faith and peace. We love you and bless you in our hearts. Sweet words. An epic moment. May God bless you and Carol always.

—Katherine Moyer—

Beloved Ken,
Wow, you are an incredible blessing to me and to us all. I have trudged through so many physical challenges by now myself, yet I keep on ticking, with ever deeper and wider gratitude. I have often wondered if my closing moments were upon me. You inspire me with your generosity and with your inspirational perspective on embracing the final graduation in this realm.

I know how unfun the nuts and bolts of physical challenges can be, and how difficult it is to watch a loved one endure them, so my heart is with Carol as she loves you on and on and on.

You are both so dear to my heart. I'll always remember your jumping off the dock into the water to rescue my baby miniature schnauzer when she fell off the edge. Thank you for being you, for sharing your beingness in life and in this glorious final journey you are on.

I love you both very much.

Katherine

—Kenny replied to Katherine—

Katherine,

I am so grateful that you have gotten value from my thoughts and words. Esther Jantzen can be thanked for encouraging me to set it up and do it more than a month ago. She is my soul sister.

I know a little about your own journey, and its challenges, and I'm glad my perspective has given you some strength and encouragement. You are such a sweet, loving doll, and I'm so glad that Carol and I got to share some very precious and unique times together with you and my Dad at the Island House on West Point Island.

I want to thank you for the very special card you sent me with photos of J-R and John and some flowers and a seed. I have had it taped to my bedroom door ever since.

Keep your focus on your Soul Tone. The Traveler will provide whatever strength you need, and will give you insights into how to handle the upcoming steps.

God bless you with great loving, and Light and peace.

I love you,

Kenny

—Loma Davidson—

Dear Ken. I just received word from Billy Whelan (who was e-mailed by Pam on the Big Island). I read your complete blog, and I admire your honesty in writing. You are a good writer. It will be very helpful to those going through illnesses and wondering about the purpose of the illness and life. God Bless you and dear Carol.

—Kenny's friend Wes Cooler—

Kenny,

I learned of your current "adventure" through the wonders of Facebook, and Cynt was kind enough to pass along your blog URL. The first reaction to learning someone we know is battling a deadly disease is always predictable—sorrow, sympathy, sadness, and a rush of good memories. Reading your blog affirms the good memories of a guy who always seemed to have it together, no matter what the situation—a guy unafraid to step off into another adventure in uncharted terrain. Most of my interactions with you were long ago, but notably included sharing in New Jersey man's first steps on the moon, and a private tour of Old Stone Church and its caretaker's quarters. I think I still have an issue of The Chronicle from Clemson featuring some of your work. As I read the words you share with us all, two things come to mind that can best be expressed in the local dialect of your hometown: "You ain't changed a bit," and "You sure do come from good people."

In recent years, I have opined that among the many things our culture has forgotten how to do is die with dignity. Like you, I was privileged to hold the hand of a parent as the solitary witness to my dad's passing. His time had come way too early, but he faced it straight on, knowing that death, like birth, is part of the package we get when we sign on to live on this incredibly wonderful and interesting little cosmic aberration we call home. Seems like you've got a good handle on that situation.

Here's wishing only the best of all that comes to you and many thanks for sharing this latest "adventure" with us all.

Until the next time, my friend,
Wes

—Kenny replied to Wes—

Hi, Wes,

Thanks for sharing your memories and thoughts so abundantly. I really appreciate being reminded of all the things you shared. And thanks for bringing some fresh insights into the meaning of all that.

Yes, I come from good people. I also "get 'er done." I do what must be done in order for God to fill in the rest. You could call it a recipe for life. I say, "God meets me at my point of action."

—Judith Johnson—

Dear and precious Ken,

Thank you for so generously sharing your heart and soul, your humor and wisdom as you continue on your journey home to the heart of God. My mom and I were abducted by hospice angels during the last few months of her life journey, and I can only hope and pray that you are as blessed by their presence as we were. May you and Carol continue to be filled, surrounded, and protected by the Light and love of our Travelers and all of us near and far who are holding you both in our hearts and prayers for your highest good. May you be blessed with peace and joy in your hearts now and forever more.

Much love,

Judith

—Kenny's friend Steve Alexander—

Kenny, just wanted to let you know some of the things that make my day.

Knowing you has been the high point of my life. The sign on my front porch that you left. The silent treatment. Don't forget the camping trip when I got home from Vietnam. And my personal favorite—go-cart racing in front of the Opel. The thing that will be with me is the love you have for everyone you meet.

We will meet again,

Steve

—Kenny responds to Steve—

Hi, Steve,

Knowing you has been very enriching for me in many, many ways. Your abiding and hilarious sense of humor has always made me want to hang around and see what country witticism was going to come up next to tickle me. Who was it that shot the arrow into the power line in front of your house?

Yes, so many precious memories that we shared. Your wonderful and loving mother, Eris, treated me like a second son, and I always appreciated it even if I didn't show it.

You will always be my friend, regardless of where we are.

When you see or hear a red-tailed hawk, think of me. That's my spirit bird.

Your buddy,
Kenny Jones

—Charlotte Liddell—

Aloha, dear Ken,

I received your call today and I was filled with the wonder of life, the matter-of-factness in your voice, the joy I heard underneath it in reading your blog—the exquisite beauty of your so many friends really being with you and cheering you on!

The love expressed in your relationship with your wife, what a life you have had to have a finale such as this! I applaud you with all my heart! I appreciate that you have been in my life and the lives of my children—know that your love carries on in the most amazing ways.

May your body find peace. May your love reverberate back to you a zillion-fold and lift you to your freedom. Thank you for being you.

—Kenny responds to Charlotte—

Charlotte,

This is a really love-filled comment you have left me. I cried all the way through it. To know that I affected your life in a way that would cause you to say such wonderful things about me was very touching and unexpected.

Because I know I did some crappy things in our relationship and with your children, but I have forgiven myself for that and forgotten about it. God bless you, Erin, Noel and Pete. I wish you all the best.

Always in loving,
Ken Jones

—Charlotte—

God bless you, Ken. You are in my thoughts, prayers, and heart. I wish you soft surrender into the bliss, my friend. Aloha and love.

Chapter 18

What's New Today?

Ken, Wednesday, March 17, 2010

I got a new hospital bed in my room, and it is so much more convenient and flexible to use than the old bed, a great and welcome addition. I can use the side rails to turn myself easier, and I can raise and lower my head and feet by myself. It's great.

Most people don't realize that about all I have left is mental energy. Today, when I tried to stand up on my own, I ran out of breath and had to sit back down. I couldn't walk for the first time.

The good news... I had a really healthy bowel movement this evening without needing an enema. I can't tell you how happy that made me and Carol. It's a big deal because my pain meds tend to put my digestive system to sleep, so something as simple as a bowel movement can become a very big problem.

Again, we asked Spirit to meet us at our point of action, so I got out of bed and on the commode and delivered. It was heavenly and I was grateful.

As I said in the beginning, I am now living on mostly mental energy, and I have to be very conservative with it. To write, to speak, to listen and respond, even to read consume my energy, and I have to recharge it. I do that with my Oxycodone, long sleeps and short naps, good food, peace and quiet, chanting my soul tone, listening to my Soul Awareness CDs, and tithing and seeding. These are the things that give me energy. Tithing is giving 10 percent of your income to the source of your spiritual teachings. Simply said, seeding is the planting of what you want to receive. To find out more, go to www.tithing.org/seeding_what.php.

When I chant my soul tone, the Mystical Traveler appears to recharge my energy. What or who is the Mystical Traveler? The one who has the ability to take me into the Soul Realm, show me the way, and remind me that I am a soul in a human body. Is that different from Jesus the Christ? No, Jesus was a Mystical Traveler. But yes, they do have somewhat different jobs. Some of you probably don't understand that or believe it. It's not up to me to define that for anybody, but if you want to know more, check it out on the MSIA website, www.msia.org.

In fact, the best thing to do, from my point of view, is subscribe to MSIA Soul Awareness Discourses to read the most profound spiritual writings on the planet. Fifty dollars for the first twelve issues is a no-brainer. If you don't get any value from it, don't renew for the second year. If you want to know the reality of God as a practical, personal, immediate, constant presence in your life, you can get it with Soul Awareness Discourses. I did. I know God and God knows me. Jesus has been my older brother since Southern Baptist summer camp in the foothills of the Blue Ridge Mountains of South Carolina when I was about twelve years old. Jesus showed me His reality at that time during a prayer by Dr. Batson at evening chapel. Shortly after that, Dr. Batson baptized me in the First Baptist Church of Pickens, South Carolina.

—————

—Mark Berson—

Kenny, your written words and thoughts have been both inspiring and meaningful. It's an interesting irony when the person whom you wish to console ends up consoling you before you ever get a word in... As I'm sure you remember, coaches always seem to get their words in somehow, so this has been unusual.

My relationship with your beautiful family has been one of the real treasures of my life. I pray for you and thank you for your strength, wisdom and character.

—End-of-Life Spiritual Advisor—

Today I woke and went immediately to the "eagle cam" to watch the mother and father bald eagles feed their three little babies. The third one, now about four days old, hatched despite the egg being laid in six inches of snow! Their little fluffball heads poke up like dandelions, and the mother and father take turns feeding them—and sometimes even each other—fish!

And so you too will always be cared for and cared about... by all whose lives that are forever interwoven with yours. You know everything you need to know, have everything you need, and you are relaxing into a sort of hammock of your caring community of friends and family.

In your own way you have already won this "battle." Even when there are no more words to say or hear, you will always be fully present and real and substantial. Rest in the gentle fullness of Spirit that surrounds you and Carol. Look to the morning. Love and sweet dreams.

Until next time...

Chapter 19

Final Days? Red-Tailed Hawk

Ken, Saturday, March 20, 2010

The nurse came last night and gave me an enema and a suppository, and I had a fine BM and feel so much better. There's a lot more to the story, but better left off.

I have become a very fussy eater, especially since seeing *Julie and Julia*. My appetite seems to be slipping, so why eat mediocre food? I got a copy of Julia Child's book on eBay and have read about French cooking in general and how to make French sauces. She is so good, and fun to read.

Today I look forward to a Hawaiian lunch of laulau, lomi-lomi salmon, and chicken long rice from the Aloha Cafe. Carol will also have a Hawaiian lunch of her choice. We will have haupia (coconut pudding, a traditional Hawaiian dish) for dessert. I also plan to have an upcoming meal from Chef Marilyn's Soul Food Express. Good Southern cookin'.

I am comfortable and happy. I finished writing my obituary last night and have made pretty much all the final arrangements for my transition into Spirit. There will be a memorial service for me here at Prana (Peace Awareness Labyrinth and Gardens) and one also in Pickens, South Carolina, for my East Coast family and friends.

My body will be cremated and the ashes spread in Barnegat Bay, New Jersey, along with some in the Atlantic Ocean in

Lavallette and Bay Head. Barnegat Bay is the beloved body of water where our Newman family had our Island House for about seventy-five years. I learned to swim, row, and sail in the bay, and I was a lifeguard at Bay Head with Capt. Bill Dowling and at Lavallette with co-guard Gordon Hesse.

Two of my sisters and I have rigged up video conferencing on our computers and have already had two video conversations, which were very nice. The third sister is still working on it. We can only do one pair of people at a time, but it's better than nothing. Of course, if they all had Mac computers and knew how to use them, we could all four video conference together at the same time. No judgment there, I'm just saying… some people like driving Toyotas and some people like driving Mercedes Benzes, that's all. Anyway, ain't technology wonderful that we can use it this way? I look forward to more video conferences in the coming days.

I have been tiring easily and quickly lately, so I have to be careful not to expend too much energy with visitors, who seem to be dropping by more frequently. Peace and quiet is what I need a lot of these days.

My spirit bird is the red-tailed hawk, so whenever you see or hear one, think of me. I have a red-tailed hawk feather in my hat band as a gift from my friend Marsha Scott. There is a red-tailed hawk living nearby that likes to eat the koi in our pond. It also likes to bathe in our rills. One day I saw it running along the side of the upper pool at Prana with its tail stuck in the water. It looked like it was playing with the water. Odd but endearing behavior. I hope to see the hawk again soon.

—Cynthia Griffith (Kenny's sister)—

I am so glad you have chosen the red-tailed hawk as your spirit bird. We have loved them since Jim and I got married and have always thought of them as a good omen for the day. It just seems right that you would choose that bird. We will always think of you when we see one.

I wanted to also let you know some of the things about you that have meant so much to me. Most of these memories are from our childhood. First I want to thank you for treating me like a person. Since I was the youngest I tried very hard to be noticed (as my family can attest). But you, Kenny, never dismissed me or ignored me and you helped me to learn lots of things. You let me tag along and were not mean to me. Thanks for not treating me like Eugenia did (ha-ha). I learned from you what a fart was. I kid you not. I still remember the very first loud fart I heard. I said, "What was that?" and everyone in the car died laughing at me and you had to explain it to me. It was a doozie.

Next, thanks for treating me like a little brother. These are some of the things you taught me, since you didn't have a little brother. How to make a noose. Your Boy Scout skills really came in handy. Then you taught me how to swing from the noose convincingly so the neighbors would have a heart attack and come running. That was a great trick. You taught me how to hold my breath for a long time and beat anyone at the Country Club swimming pool. You convinced me to dive off the high dive at Table Rock. Very scary. You taught me how to bicycle without holding the handlebars. I did great until... well, I still have the scar on my knee. You taught me how to do a flip on the trampoline. You were very patient and did not make fun of me. You taught me how to do a lay-up in the backyard in our dirt court. I could not get my steps right, but finally you made me understand and we practiced together. But I did not get the jump shot. Oh well, sometimes I failed. You taught me to love rock and roll and FM radio. You and Mom taught me how to body surf in the waves. We had so much fun.

I also want to thank you for treating me like a girl. You brought the entire Clemson swim team home for Debbie and me to pick from. That was an awesome brother! Then you introduced us to all of the Lavallette lifeguards. You were the best!

You were the ringleader for the mob at the beach when we pretended to be the hillbillies from the sticks. Sidney B. Zorch and his sisters. Mom and Dad were not surprised but laughed right along with us.

I wanted you to know some of the fun things about you that I cherish and will remember to tell my grandchildren. Thanks for making us laugh all of our lives.

Your loving sister,

Cynt

—Kenny replied—

Well, we certainly had a lot of fun and were able to make up a lot of fun things to do on the spot. I'm glad I made a positive impact on your life. I loved you the moment Mom revealed your little baby self in the hospital bed with her when you were just a few hours old, and I have ever since. Seeing you so new in the world made you a precious sister and gave me a protective responsibility that I embraced you in.

I love you dearly.

Your brother,

Kenny

—Georgea Muschel—

I think I overstayed my visit today because there was so much sweet, precious energy in the room that I didn't want to leave. Ken and Carol, you are both amazing and so loving. Even at this time, Ken, your humor and light and generosity of spirit shines through so strongly I forget how weak your body is and all that you are going through. God Bless you. I love you very much.

—Carol wrote to Kenny's sister Debbie today—

Dear Debbie,

Your sentiments are beautiful and go deep to my soul. Kenny talks about his condition openly and with a lot of love and respect for his process. He loves you very much.

As for our marriage, we have had many challenges over the years, differences in approach to many things, but when this diagnosis hit us, all the negative aspects of our relationship melted away, leaving our pure love and devotion strong and palpable. We are basking in such loving that I have never known before. Kenny will have his own take on this, but for me, I am doing what I know how to do best and leaving all the rest to God to orchestrate. So many times in the last few months as one crisis after another has loomed, we prayed out loud for Spirit (God) to fill the gaps and every time it has done so. The most important aspect of this is Kenny's ability to set clear intentions that Spirit can recognize and muster his strength as needed time and time again. He's amazing. My hero, showing me how to access Spirit even in the most challenging circumstances. I thank God for every day, hour, minute, and second we have together.

God bless you, Debbie.

Love you,

Carol

—End-of-Life Spiritual Advisor—

Okay, so here's a song that is not exactly about a red-tailed hawk spirit bird, but I think it is really meant to be!

"They that wait upon the Lord will renew their strength. They will rise up on wings as eagles" (Isaiah 40:31).

"On Eagles Wings"
by Michael Joncas

Speaking of the shelter of the Lord as our refuge and our rock in whom we trust, here is the last stanza.
And He will raise you up on eagle's wings,
Bear you on the breath of dawn,
Make you to shine like the sun,
And hold you in the palm of His hand.
And hold you in the palm of His hand.

—Robert Peake—

Ken, it was precious to spend some time with you this evening. I wrote about the experience on my own blog: http://www.robertpeake.com/archives/1003-blogging-the-end-that-is-the-beginning.html. I titled it "Blogging the End that is the Beginning." Here is what I wrote:

Tonight Val and I got to spend some time with Ken Jones, a friend of ours who was also a fellow resident during the nearly four years I lived in the seminary. He is now receiving hospice care in his room, lovingly supported by his wife. When we entered the room, he was arranging a music play list for his memorial service from his hospital bed, his glowing MacBook Pro resting on the over-bed table. Ken has also been blogging about his journey with cancer, and what now seem likely to be his final days with us in this world.

Western writing often treats death in fiction, but rarely have I read the words of an author knowingly in their final stage of life. Yet there is a longstanding tradition in Zen, practiced by monks and samurai alike, of writing death poems. The best of these poems capture the essence of one's life, turning an aesthetic and philosophical gaze upon the often taboo subject of death. It occurs to me that this is similar to what Ken is doing with his blog.

More than this, spending time with Ken, he seemed to me to have become a living poem. When it began to look more likely that his time here would come to an end, Ken says he asked God to grant him "some extra time to be of service to anyone I can in any way I can." I was served by Ken's presence tonight, which seemed to have with it a radiance that I also recall in the final moments we spent with our son.

Ken's message is simple and profound: "We are here in this material world for a relatively short time for our education and opportunities to be of service to others through our loving. The better we do that, the more fun our lives will be. Having fun is a big key to successful living. If it doesn't seem like fun at any moment, find a way to make it fun. I guess that's my message. Have fun with your lives."

Thank you, Ken, for your example, your friendship, your fun. You have indeed been of service to me through your writing and your presence. My love goes out to you and your sweet wife, Carol.

All I can say right now is thank you.

<hr />

"Kenny"
By Jennifer Halet

Kenny's a friend, a man noble and strong,
In the line of the Travelers, so loving and long.
He's a unique Soul, gentle, kind, and sweet,
Even with that nasty bullwhip lying at his feet,
From the wisdom of my Soul, what I truly do know
Is that Ken's one of our brightest lights, constantly aglow.
Once in a class trio, I faced the demons of my past,
And Ken and Carol radiated loving until the very last.
Ken, I saw your love and compassion through my tears.
Because of you, a healing courage overcame my fears.
Lesser men might have judged me; maybe run and flee,
Your loving acceptance helped set me free.
Your silent ministry, this quiet act
Allowed me to ground a new freedom, with strength intact.
It's interesting how we walk upon this earth,
So blindly unaware of our own true worth.
My sense of value has grown more each day;
Thank you, God bless you—what can I really say?
Through the years, unbeknownst to you,
I've listened to your wisdom because it rings so true.
Kenny, you've helped me open to a greater Love.
When I've fallen, you reached out from above.
I learned my loved ones I so terribly did miss
Are always here, comforting me with their Divine kiss.

Kenny, you're dependable and true,
yet still catch us by surprise.
As Carmen Miranda at Conference,
you had us rolling in the aisle.
As I enjoy this moment, so precious and rare;
I'm happy to know that Ken is always nearby somewhere.
Yesterday I saw the good and the God in your eyes,
Shining radiantly through our laughter and our cries.
Your twinkle said, "Oh yes, it's all true!
"Now how you live your life is up to you."
With integrity and goodness you live your life,
I see the love and consideration in how you honor your wife.
Yes, you and Carol have true love,
Manifesting on this level, what is so from above.
Now I'm encouraged, not jaded in matters of the heart,
Thanks to you, I don't use a hardness to keep apart.
Like a red-tail hawk, Kenny, you always do soar,
Confidently inspiring us to go for far more.
So in each moment, the Traveler says, "All Aboard!"
What a joyful blessing to know we're always with the Lord.

—Lynda Reece Sentell Stevenson—

Kenny (you will always be "Kenny" to me)

I can't begin to tell you how much I admire how you approach your "final days" with such dignity and courage (not to mention a fine sense of humor). You are an inspiration to both me and my husband. We identify with and celebrate your decision to enter the Spirit world with dignity intact. I join with your wife in shouting out to this world, "You are my Hero!" My hope for you today is that you see the red-tailed hawk! I trust you will.

Lynda

The Blessing

Dear Lord and all of Your creation, we bring ourselves before You to the holy place, that You have contacted us in the consciousness of the soul.

We ask that You open up our individual consciousnesses so that we may have Your truth and love revealed to us and that we may expand our ability to comprehend and understand.

We give thanks for the consciousness we call the Christ and the Mystical Traveler. We appreciate that the opportunity is rarefied, as many are called but few choose back.

And what does it matter how many have chosen when each one You have chosen meets up directly with You? In Your consciousness, You take each one in completely, such that each of us becomes the Beloved. And as You are the way, each one chosen by You becomes the way and the truth and the Light.

Those of us who are gathered together as the Beloved and who, for now, remain in this world give thanks for Your protection, for Your strength, and for knowing the purpose that is the soul. We are here to fulfill the spiritual promise. We are here creating through grace, the grace of the Beloved. Baruch Bashan.

—John Morton, *You Are the Blessings*

Chapter 20

The Blessings Already Are

Ken, March 22, 2010

Almost anything I could ask Spirit for at this point seems to already be provided. There may be some things I could ask for…

I am visualizing reduced swelling in my legs, and healing of some damaged tissue in my body.

I visualize grace and ease with my next bowel movement.

I visualize having enough energy to be present with my family and friends these days.

Getting delicious and nutritious foods at each meal would be nice too.

—————

—Debbie Robinson (Kenny's sister)—

Kenny,

When we were on the video call, you told me someone had brought you hyacinths and they smelled so good. The next day, I went outside in my yard and my hyacinths were in full bloom. I had not seen them before, and I felt a very strong connection to you when I picked and smelled them. I will always think of you when I see them now.

I read Cynthia's comments. She is right about the advantages of having an older brother. There were so many things we dared to try, but we had fun just playing softball, football, tetherball, basketball. One thing I learned from you was never pick a fight with someone who was a lot bigger! I learned much more than that, of course, but that one was a shocker for me—all you had to do was put your hand on my forehead with your arm out straight and I couldn't hit or kick you, much to my disappointment.

I have read all the other beautiful comments that people have made and I am so grateful you have been able to share in their thoughts and memories. You are very blessed.

I love you, my brother.

Debbie

—Ashley and Jason—

Dear Ken,

Thank you so much for sharing your process with us. We admire you and your peace and courage now and even before. You and Carol have blessed our lives and we are so thankful to be your friends. We love you and wish you much comfort and relaxation. Thank you for showing us what is truly important.

—Kathleen Safron—

Dear Ken,

Thank you sooo much for this beautiful and honest blog. I am so touched by the depth of your being. You have so served me, and I am utterly grateful.

I am sending you and Carol much love and Light. I can feel how you are being held in the arms of the Travelers.

Love,
Kathleen

—Tamsin Rothschild—

Hi, Ken and Carol

I hope you get this message. I was not sure how else to get in touch with you. I have been sending Light every day to you both and just wanted to send my love, and good cheer. May you both be balmed in God's abundant glow now, and each day and moment as you move forward. I see much vivid white light all around you. God bless you, and if there is anything I can do, please don't hesitate to ask. With all my love, Tamsin

—Lisa Peake—

Dearest Ken,

You are the blessings! Thank you from the depths of my heart for sharing yourself with us.

Your sweet presence at Prana is one of my favorite memories of living there, bumping into you while I made toast in the kitchen.

I'm sending you Light and loving and seeing you filled with joy, delighting in your delicious food, and the sweet loving care of Carol and your nearest and dearest.

Carol, you are a Spiritual Warrior like none other, and I love and honor you. Bless you both, you are in my prayers every day. I am filled with such gratitude for you both.

In loving,
Lisa

—Cheryl Luft—

Ken, I was diagnosed with breast cancer last December. I have appreciated your sharing. Today I am visiting Sedona, and I saw two red-tail hawks. I wish I could have pulled the car over to see what they were doing, as they seemed quite active with each other. Nonetheless, I did think of you with wings!

Fly well, with Light.

Many Blessings, Cheryl

—Janet Volasko, wife of Baja
Nutri-Care fellow cancer patient—

Dearest Ken and Carol

My beloved John passed March 6 surrounded with pure love from our children, my best friend, and his favorite nurses. John passed with a big tear in his eye as he really did not want to leave us so soon. I take great comfort that his angels started gathering the night before as he said they keep calling him, and he could see us from above. My son said it was the morphine speaking, but I know otherwise. Kenny, can you find John and take him sailing? He would love that. Carol, stay strong. I am with you in prayer.

Janet

—Cynthia Collier (Kenny's second wife)—

Ken, I always loved your spontaneity and sense of adventure, and we did have so many great adventures together... from river rafting to running a wilderness company to car camping all around the country in some unexpected places (like a golf course, which we realized early in the a.m. when the sprinklers went off!) Time does fly, doesn't it, my friend? And it seems you are on a beautiful new river that is taking you gracefully into more expansion and tender loving and the beautiful art of letting go... thank you for sharing your process... it is a gift to us all, and we love you for being who you are.

Cynthia

Chapter 21

What's da Haps?

Ken, March 24, 2010

Having lived on Kauai for six years, I learned that's how Hawaiians say, "What's happening now?"

Today I am having Carol take dictation.

Yesterday was an interesting day. Let's call it my "pie day." I had one friend show up with my favorite coconut custard pie—a whole one—from Urth Caffe. They make the best coconut custard pie on earth.

I shared it with five friends. It was fantastic. Before we could even finish, another friend showed up with a whole apple pie from Apple Pan. They make the best apple pie in the world. Plus a pint of Häagen-Dazs vanilla. They make the best vanilla ice cream in the world. So I had apple pie and ice cream following the coconut custard. After that my consciousness was such a blur I can't remember if I ate any dinner or not. But I do remember having a gratifying bowel movement afterward.

Today I had a wonderful video conference with my sister Cynthia, some wonderful e-mails from friends and family, wonderful phone calls and visits from friends, some great naps, a wonderful bath, and great value from the Circle of Light provided by the Heartfelt Foundation.

Among the many community services Heartfelt provides the Los Angeles area, they organize comfort and care for members of MSIA who are close to making their transition leaving behind the physical body. This describes the Circle of Light.

Today I listened to my favorite musician, Mark Knopfler's, latest album *Get Lucky*. Knopfler is such an extraordinary musician, storyteller, and guitar player with an extremely wide repertoire of musical styles. Seems I never get tired of his music.

As usual, Carol's been taking extraordinary care of me today in every way and being an adorable doofus. Looking forward to more pie later.

———

—Celia Allen-Graham—

Hi, Ken,

Love your blog, your Spirit, your sense of humor, and especially your knowing who you are! You are a blessing to us all. Light and loving to you and Carol

I love you, my friend.

All ways, happy traveling!

Celia

—Charles Bernstein—

Dearest Ken,

Serving you as a Circle of Lighter yesterday was about as easy as eating pie! it was so wonderful to sit with you in your room, see that amazing Light coming through your eyes, watching how lovingly Carol takes care of your every need...

Now I'm gonna check out red-tailed hawks.

I continue to hold you and Carol so very dearly in my heart.

Charles

—Jacquelyn Rone—

Hi, Ken,

The pie was an extra treat, but the best was getting to visit with you! What a demonstration you are of being the spiritual observer and enjoying life to the fullest. Your joy and enthusiasm is a blessing to me.

Love always,
Jacquelyn

—End-of-Life Spiritual Advisor—

Dear Kenny and Carol,

I guess I might need to change your name from "peaceful warrior" to "the coconut custard pie warrior," which brings to mind a whole different range of entertaining possibilities.

Today it was raining hard and blowing in huge gusts, so I checked the eagle cam online to see what on earth was happening with the three little bald head eaglets.

I found the mother using her wings as an umbrella, protecting her young (not even two weeks old) from the unrelenting elements. Her head bowed over them, keeping them warm. It is a powerful image of God's particular love for us all, and you are a living testimony to the tender care and love possible when offered and received. They get fish gently fed to them, but alas no coconut pie or apple pie with ice cream! Thank you for spending some energy letting us know how you are doing. Until next time, With love.

—Alexandra Roberts—

Hi beautiful Ken,

Just discovered this wonderful blog and what tenderness to see and to immerse myself in. You and Carol are so loved. As a member of Circle of Light, it is very sacred being here for both of you.

This Circle of Light being held is indeed expansive and embracing.

Beloved love and Light to you both, Alexandra

Chapter 22

The Day My Dear Friend Kevin Helped Me Fill out the Mortuary Forms

Carol writes...

It was March 23, 2010, just seven days before Kenny passed into Spirit, when Kevin and I sat together in the small seminar room, the most ornate and timeless room in the house. Originally the family dining room, replete with cherubs, soldier-like figures, rams' heads, swans, and fruits and vegetables emblazoned in every media; carved gold-gilt walnut, cast polychrome cornicing, oils on canvas, and hammered brass, this room is now appreciated by many ministers and students of the Mystical Traveler in classes and meetings.

This time, the cherubs and soldiers and all the rest watched over us as we combed through the mortuary forms indicating what I wanted done with Kenny's "remains." Remains? How cold and unfeeling, that word, "remains." He was still with us! And here I was filling out forms for when he was dead.

Two weeks had passed since my beloved husband decided to enlist hospice care. Some people, I hear, last quite a long time in hospice. Some even get better. But we knew Kenny's days were numbered because he would have to stop receiving blood transfusions in hospice, and without blood transfusions, he would get weaker each day until there was no more energy to breathe. And so it was, just nineteen days after his last transfusion, on

March 30, he breathed his last breath surrounded by loved ones and welcomed by a chorus of angels and family who had gone before him to usher him into the Realms of the Divine.

But there he was down the hall still receiving visitors with enthusiasm, still smiling his forever smile, and still eating his favorite foods like Hawaiian laulau, lomi-lomi salmon, and chicken long rice from the Aloha Café, with haupia for dessert. There he was, enjoying every visitor who came to share their loving. There he was basking in his morning bath, no complaints really. Oh maybe a pain when he was turned in bed or maybe the swelling in this feet hurt a bit, but I'm convinced now as I look back on the images I have held all these days, weeks, and months that the absence of pain was measured by and due to the exquisite and palpable love and gratitude he was emanating and giving and receiving and expounding upon whenever anyone asked.

And I am meant to fill out these forms while he is living the most profound days of his life 200 percent? How unfair! We weren't prepared, largely due to my resistance to the inevitable. But that's another story—how denial serves and how it undermines the beauty and sacredness of the truth.

I couldn't bear doing it alone, nor could I bear to be away from Kenny, except to do little tasks that only took a minute or two. But this task was gargantuan. My heart and throat ached, and I couldn't stop the tears with every sentence I read and every mark I made. Dear Kevin read with me, helped me focus, and poured out his love and compassion with the tone of his voice, with his clarity of mind, sitting real close with his full attention and his presence and his willingness—to just sit with me and hold while I wrote and checked boxes and barely grasped the meaning, not wanting to dwell on what happens to a body when it stops living. I can still feel enveloped in a cocoon of caring, the kind of caring that really works—to ease the burden, to console the tears, to hold all of me, all levels of consciousness in the love of the Spiritual Heart. Try as I might throughout all these chapters to describe the wondrous moments when I was acutely aware of the presence of Spirit, I can only hope these word pictures touch you enough to reach your heart and give you a sense of their power, their sweetness, their unpredictable magnitude.

And here we are, another day in a life when one of us has met his last day in the glory that God prepares for us. Through my words, my pioneer tracker husband is still showing those of us reaching the age when we contemplate our own mortality more seriously—that we can leave this world with the truth on our lips and in our hearts, knowing we are one with God and welcoming the ascension to which we are all heir—into the Heart of God.

God bless you and remember to prepare those papers ahead of time so it's all taken care of when the time comes that one of you will lift off before the other.

—Millicent—

Hello darling Carol,

I read the latest blog about the papers. Although I did not see a husband die, I was witness to a marriage dying and my own death of what was the only life I knew—as a wife, mother, daughter, grandmother, and all the Jewish stuff. I know the experience of death and dying very well! For me it has been a long process of letting go and allowing God/Spirit to lead me according to His will, not mine. Not an easy task. It is not an emotion but real love filling me that comes present.

You are so touched with Spirit when you write. Kenny was/is wonderful and continues to enlighten. I am so very proud of you for reaching to those places so very hard to get to. You too are wonderful in my eyes and an inspiration for others. God bless you, beloved one. Keep writing as many are open to healing through your words.

Chapter 23

Six Breaths, and I Can Stay Alive

Carol remembers...

In the last couple of days before he died, my darling Kenny discovered if he breathed six conscious breaths in a row, he could keep himself alive longer. He asked me what I thought of doing the six breaths. I found myself telling him he could do it however he wanted to—to me that meant he could do the breaths and stay alive longer, or he could just breathe normally. At every turn I possibly could, I tried not to influence his decisions about his health, his treatment, or his quality of life or death. But inside me I was screaming, please, please don't go, don't leave me. This theme has played out too many times in my life—please don't leave me.

The hospice material outlined the signs that death was near in terms of weeks and days and hours. These didn't fit Kenny's signs, which had been obvious for several months as I looked back to compare. So each day as he got weaker and weaker, it was never apparent to me that any day would be the last day, not until the last few hours. I'm pretty sure I can attribute how long he sustained those signs to his personal strength, his undeniable awareness that Spirit was breathing him, and the previous months of physical cleansing and strengthening.

If there's anything worth remembering in this message, it's to get close, spend lots of time looking into your loved one's eyes, and listening to their words, their prayers, their unspoken and spoken questions, and consciously pour as much love as you can into each gesture, each task, each response, each touch, each communication. And if you feel the calling to stay close, follow that. In the last week, I only left the room to get some food once a day or so for only a few minutes at a time.

I remember telling someone that I would have given Kenny some of my years if I could. Their reply, "Maybe you did."

In all of this I am comforted to know I did the best I could with what I knew how to do to take as good care of my husband as I possibly could. Do I have any regrets now? Oh yes, I wish I could have been more conscious, more responsive, more present, more a lot of things. But there's a karmic flow to everything and we were in one that had its own limitations and parameters. Within this flow, I am grateful for all the assistance from people on this side of the veil and all the Masters of Light and souls on the other side who lighted the way for my beloved.

Fly home, Kenny. See you in the Soul Realm.

Carol

March 16, 2010, phone consultation with healer Dr. Edward Wagner

Kenny's Basic Self picked up on someone else's panic about Kenny passing. It was Carol's. Kenny is instructed to disconnect from Carol's panic, which was tied to a past lifetime when Kenny died and would wander as a ghost because he did not get a proper burial. Carol has a memory of fear and upset.

Kenny is clearing up karma from many lifetimes, and the pain he suffered in his body is a balancing act for the pain he caused other people in their bodies—a number of lifetimes were involved.

Ed instructs Kenny to take a breath and let it all go. The etheric realm negativity being released is seeking to turn Kenny from transcendence to abandonment. It actually did this in another life. Forgive all this and let it go.

The dark lord of the etheric realm pushed on your attitude. You were deceived and went into despair which blocks you from the greater light. Don't do that again. Don't feed it.

March 20, 2010, another consultation with Ed Wagner

Ed intuits that Kenny took drugs in the past. The right heart meridian and soul meridian are blocked. The line goes from the pubic bone to the lip, and then the upper lip, over the head and down the spine.

The right side is remembering the death that lasted five minutes under hallucinatory effect. Ed intuits that Kenny has three hallucinatory detached or dissociated entities. When on the drug trip, they left his body, leaving a hole in the mouth and causing damage to the heart meridian at the soul level. These entities believe they are the real you. By your doing hallucinatory drugs, you were saying you didn't want to be you, so they're trying to fulfill that request—to imprint the thought that calls you to the other side to join them.

However, they are not on the other side. They are still in the hallucination. We need to draw them back into you, heal them, and reintegrate them back into you, because they can't just be dispelled. So Carol is to tap up and down the spine to help the reintegration process. Call them. Say, "I call these dispelled, detached hallucinatory entities of mine back into the body," and then Carol taps again. Ed sees them being healed as gas coming out of the mouth and tells Kenny to do the same. See them integrated into you so you are restored to that time prior to taking drugs. Say, "I've integrated you back into me to be restored to that time prior to LSD and mushrooms."

March 25, 2010, another consultation with Ed Wagner

Ed sees that Kenny has inherited a lack of spiritual chi. He sees a tremendous loss over no animal connection to his soul. He sees Kenny's consciousness experiencing a loss over not having enough contact with nature. The soul is deprived on these three levels: no family connection to the soul, no animal contact, and no nature contact. Plus there is an autoimmune response to life (which probably contributed to tendency toward cancer). Electrical currents of the nervous system became allergic to electrical currents of life. The thyroid gland was effected by this (became cancerous in 2002 and was removed). Carol is instructed to tap Kenny's spine, and he is instructed to release these effects and pray that these false programs are removed and he is restored to the level as if he had grown up in spiritually focused circumstances.

March 29, 2010, one day before Kenny passed into Spirit, last consultation with Ed Wagner

Gacky (Kenny's paternal grandfather) is here. He came for you, Kenny, and he will help you.

Ed senses that Kenny is concerned about breaking Carol's heart. This is his time, Ed says. Gacky said from the deepest level, it's time for Kenny's sisters and Carol to let him go.

Carol, you are to place your hands on his forehead and abdomen—and he is to release all worry about any broken hearts, minds, and souls of his three sisters and you that would take place from his passing. Gacky's been with Kenny for three days. There's nothing more to heal, he says. You just need to know you're not leaving any negative imprints or harm on anyone. This is complete liberation. Everybody's okay with letting you go. He wants Ken to completely give in to peace, to fuse with Spirit. Completely let go into God's arms and mind. Meditate that Gacky is there. Your passing is going to be an incredibly peaceful and satisfying sense of completion of your soul. Ed says Kenny's fortunate to have Gacky there. We are to place a photo of Gacky on Kenny's left side as a reminder of who's there to catch him.

Ed says Ken was blessed to have Divine eyes called by God. That he is now protected from family dynamics, and he'll understand everything really soon.

Message from Kenny through Carol's writing:

November 30, 2010, eight months after Kenny passed over …
  One year after driving home from Baja Nutri-Care Clinic in
Baja, Tijuana

> *My Sweetie Wife, I'll love you forever. I even like you*
> *now! Your tears still touch my soul with compassion.*
> *I couldn't match the level of love I received from you*
> *then. But now I give you more than a life's worth. Take*
> *it in through your breath and let me swim in your soft*
> *embrace. Bye for now.*

Chapter 24

We Were Counting Breaths 'til the Last One

Carol writes...

It was the night Kenny took his last breath. My Circle of Light fellow ministers were standing by in our bedroom and in the hall outside, silently meditating and ushering in Kenny's passing. Each in our own way knew the moment was near.

It started early in the evening, his labored breathing. I gave him some morphine and sat him up in bed to help him breathe better, but this didn't help much. He wasn't able to talk by this time, so I thought he had become unresponsive. I called hospice and they told me to administer more morphine to calm his breathing and that they would send a nurse by to check on him.

The nurse arrived and told me the time was near and that his labored breathing was part of the process. In my limited understanding, I asked again if he should be so uncomfortable, and the nurse, sensing my alarm, relented and told me to give him more morphine and another kind of sedative to calm him down.

Kenny spit the sedative out, and I dutifully put it back in his mouth. He gestured and moaned at this point, and I thought he was incoherent and agitated, which can happen according to what I had read. So without questioning or even thinking much, I gave him the morphine anyway, hoping it would calm him. He bit down on the dropper and again I just thought he was incoherent.

We both hushed a bit and fell asleep for a while, while our Circle of Light ministers were meditating silently.

At some point, just as was predicted by John Morton, I was called awake. I had been holding Kenny's hand, and then I put my other arm around his shoulders, came very close, and told him how much I loved him and it was okay to let go and to go with the Traveler. In just a few seconds, he breathed his last breath.

I think I wrote about this most precious moment in a previous post, but now I have much more understanding about who it was in me who couldn't let my husband die the way he would have liked to go, for it is obvious to me now, after replaying this scene in my mind nearly every day, that all his gesturing and moaning and refusing medication was meant to say please leave him alone in these his last moments on earth—to let him breathe his last breath consciously. Yet in those moments of panic, I reacted out of a place within myself that wanted him to be comfortable. Nice thought, but not on the right page. Why not? I reacted out of limited mindset instead of responding to the signals that were present.

This scene has played itself out in my memories over and over with no resolution, only a very painful example of my own shortcomings, my lack of awareness, my shortsighted, made-up mindset about what his death should look like. I know—that's a harsh description of my own limitations, and to this day I regret not asking him earlier what he would have liked as he was dying. I had no clue it would even be possible to ask, and he had no clue to offer what he would have liked either.

Perfectly matched in our fears of losing each other. This was definitely a characteristic of our relationship. Now it's obvious as I look back over the years of his acting out in fear and my reacting in fear. There's plenty more to say about the patterns that have been revealed to me since Kenny died, but not in this chapter.

The most important message here is what I heard Kenny say today. He told me, "You gave me so much even though you don't think so—that the least I could do was give you a moment of peace before I left. That was the only thing I could give you, my darling one."

Having heard this precious communication today, I was finally somewhat relieved of my burden and ready to write this chapter. So there's not so much blame and self-judgment left, and much more gratitude for the precious moments I experienced of Kenny's appreciation and love toward me. I cried my eyes out as I opened myself to receive his love—nine months later. Better now than never!

And just like he said would happen, our relationship grows deeper, more loving, and more intimate as I seek to reach up into the high realms to meet his soul there. The same skills, discipline, love, and letting go are required of me as those needed to experience my own soul. Imagine our radiant forms, vibrating light, radiating love, compassion, oneness, understanding, and acceptance—the most precious attributes of the soul and of any relationship. Breathe in Kenny's loving. Breathe out my loving to him. That's a very peaceful and compassionate exercise. A beautiful way to reach up.

So if (when) you hold the Light for a loved one who is dying, ask all the questions you can think of that would help make your loved one's experience the best it can be—what he or she wants it to be. I did the best I could with what I had—and you will too.

November 25, 2010, eight months after passing

Dearest Kenny,

I'm thinking about those last hours of your life on earth and how you were trying to tell us something. What was it?

Kenny: Oh Carol, it doesn't matter. Yes, you are right—I tried, but I was too far gone to do it. No morphine—yes, but I understood you needed to not see me suffer. But I wasn't suffering, I was saying how much I loved you and honored you and adored you. And I knew how sensitive you were to me and cherished every conscious moment we could have. Even though I was not breathing right, I wanted to feel you with me. And in the end you were right there ushering me into the next world, the high realms of Spirit. I picked you right from the start because in my heart I knew I didn't have long to live and that you would make miracles happen just through your perseverance and desire to please. I love you for that. I adore your sweet heart and your kindness and all the ways you loved me so much that it hurt every day. I could see the hurt and it endeared you to me like a darling little girl, my little girl. My sweetheart, my one and only lover. All those times I gave in to my addictions, I'm sorry for that and know you forgive me. I couldn't stop—too much static, not enough willpower. Gotta go, my sweet Valentine.

—From our End-of-Life Spiritual Advisor—

Dear Carol,

Thank you for posting this one too. Several things come to mind.

1. We don't get to choose how we die, really. Our bodies are all different. Being youngish, his physical body was internally stronger than some elderly people's are. I remember the anguish watching a young person try to die—in his or her mid–twenties, for instance. The internal organs have trouble shutting down. Sometimes folks linger because they are enjoying the presence of loved ones' energies. But there is a limit as to how long the

physical body, the brain, the circulation, or the kidneys can support that cycle of living. We all do have a limit. We are finite—the hardest thing for all of us to accept.

2. Shutting down is a normal process, and you saw what it looks like. The agonal breathing with gaping mouth and sounds is a physiological—not emotional suffering—process.

3. Neither you nor Kenny (having not experienced this with each other before) could be held accountable for knowing how to do one bit better.

4. The nurse's responsibility is to help you know you did exactly what you were supposed to do to help him. Morphine relaxes the person enough to where he or she doesn't experience the sense of drowning due to buildup of fluids and/or lack of oxygen. I think we talked about this part some before, but you were too fresh from the experience to take any of it in—totally understandable!

5. You got to where you both needed to be to let go. There is no "right" or "wrong" in dying any more than there is in being born.

6. I think the oral medications may have a bitter taste. It is more likely that he simply didn't like the taste. As I remember he was very particular about what tasted good and what did not! I suspect he probably was communicating that rather than some deeper desire to have a different experience than you were offering him. You helped him relax enough to let go. The end, regardless of how spiritually evolved a person is, can be a terrifying time—a giant leap of faith.

7. You stayed near. You got to be part of this. Often people cannot leave their body with someone physically near and will wait until they leave the room. Even though at that time we sense they are not physically in the body, but rather hovering above it, they know when we are near.

Kenny knew you were near, and even though you dozed off for a time, you got the very best of this experience.

8. Let go of how it happened because that is how it happens for almost everyone I have known and seen—some two thousand. Keep reminding yourself that you did your very best and even more than most are able to do.

9. Your fear takes nothing away from sharing this holy transition. It's okay to have been afraid. It did not make you less of a loving human being, less of a companion, less of a spiritual "warrior." It is tough. No way to get around that.

It's hard not to go back over it and over it, but try to take walks and smile at all you see. He will be around, smiling back! Love you.

—Carol Beau—

Carol, I am sincerely touched by your sharing, and have taken in deeply your wisdom regarding those last moments with a loved one. The sweetness and honesty of your words are comforting and have brought me to a gentler consciousness. I offer my Light for your journey.

With the loving of my heart, Carol.

Fast-Forward

December 25, 2011

Cousin Nicky will die tomorrow. His passing is quite different from Kenny's. Fraught with a lot of pain from the cancer and the ravages of chemotherapy. The family is stressed, worried, upset in so many ways. I am there to help in any way I can.

I write to Kenny: *Merry Christmas, Kenny. Missing you and reliving your last hours wishing I knew more about how to be with Nicky, Anna, and Teresa.*

Kenny says: My darling sweetie, you're doing just fine, hanging back while your ministry is working. And don't you worry about me—I needed that solitude to be able to lift off just like I needed you to let me go. See how fast I went after you let me go? Everybody was assembled on the threshold. I could see and feel them all. My entire lineage was waiting. Once I got there I recognized them all from one lifetime or another, I could understand everything in my life from the perspective of my soul. My family, my addictions and why. My successes, the beautiful expression of peace and compassion that people in this life remarked on, the tremendous love I have for you and why I chose you to usher me in my last years and days. I also understood all my failed relationships in an instant. One tableau told the whole story.

This is what Nick is experiencing right now, and I can see the Traveler has him close to its breast, breathing for him as he lets go into the tunnel of love and mercy. There's no need to worry or have concerns. Everything is on schedule. And your job is different than when you were with me. No regrets, no misunderstandings, just hold in the purity of your heart. That's your mission here.

Remember the sweetness and the dear moments we had. Let go of regrets and wishing you were different. You have many more years to do things differently from what you've learned. I adore you, I bless you every day, and I miss your touch—hold Valentine Tiger some more and I will feel it. I'm glad you're eating good stuff at Annabelle's. Prana food is boring. Give me a graham cracker!

Your devoted and forever husband, Kenny Bo.

Q: If we have a Soul inside us that is perfect, and if we started off perfect before we came here to this planet, why do we have to go through this "hell" so that we can go through these experiences, so that we can progress, so that we can go back and be perfect?

A: The Soul's being perfect does not equate to the Soul's being experienced. If being here were based upon the Soul's perfection, then the Soul would not be here to start with. But the Soul's job is to gain experience, and one of the ways it can do that is by coming here.

The Soul is to gain experience and become a co-creator with God. Perfection does not necessarily know how to create.

It is a being state. It also does not necessarily know right-wrong configurations; it sees these situations only as a perfection in the whole.

—John-Roger, Fulfilling Your Spiritual Promise

Chapter 25

Last Days

Carol, March 31, 2010

Dear friends, loved ones,

Carol here: my darling Kenny went home to God last night at 11:24 p.m. Pacific time. The last day was kind of rough. His breathing was labored and halted, which I had read was normal at end of life. But it got worse, so I called the hospice nurse to get some advice. She told me what to do, and after another bit of time Kenny relaxed some but not completely. By then a nurse had arrived to help us some more. We gave him more morphine and Ativan and atropine until his breathing slowed down. At this point I dozed a bit without realizing and when I woke up, I sat close and began telling Kenny it was okay to let go and ride on the spiral up into God's arms. After only a few more breaths he stopped breathing and was gone from this world.

And so just as John Morton counseled me, I was called awake at the right moment to utter the last words Kenny would hear before he lifted off. I am so grateful and so deeply touched he chose me to be at his side. Perhaps he was waiting for me to be able to say those words and really mean it. As I recall the image of my arm around Kenny's shoulders and my other hand holding his, those words came from somewhere other than my mind. I do believe who I really am was speaking, soul to soul.

Many friends and family sent condolences, including these.

—Celia—

Hi, Carol,

Blessing of Light, grace, ease, and rest going your way. And of course blessings of Light to my soul brother, Ken, flying very high, and free, I'm sure. You are both an "on-this-planet" example of how aware and beautiful a transition can be.

Thank you.

I love you.

—Kenny's cousins—

Kenny's spirituality and practical resilience grew through years of courageous practice. Those attributes and you, Carol, served him well.

We are sad because of his loss, yet glad because of his life.

Cam and Angela

Chapter 26

How Am I Doing?

Carol: April 2, 2010

Okay, this may be the last entry in sweet Kenny's blog or not. Maybe I'll get to tell you I saw him in the resident red-tailed hawk.

Patti Rayner, director of Heartfelt, wrote asking how I am.

I wrote back, thanks for asking, Patti. I've been sleeping a lot. Saw Bryan McMullen (chiropractor) this morning. That was good. Have some extreme fatigue in my upper back and shoulders and heart. It was good to get out of the room for a while. All the hospice equipment was taken away yesterday so that's a relief. But the room is so chaotic and I don't know how to use anyone's help. I just need to go through it one surface at a time. Going to the Walking in the Light workshop tomorrow. Jennifer Halet will drive me. Then Muriel Merchant will meet me and be my buddy for the weekend. I'm grateful for that because I'm a little skittish about being around a lot of people.

Been sending thank-you notes all night. It's helpful to keep my mind busy else it wanders into regrets and sadness and mourning. Mourning is okay except it's so painful. I keep muttering it's not fair. We didn't have enough time together in the precious glory we found once the diagnosis was pronounced. But, alas, these nine months have been more precious than lifetimes could be, with Spirit noticeably present every day in our gratitude, our compassion, our caring, our appreciation, our prayers, and our patience and trust that Spirit would provide. And it did, time and time again.

The doctors were right, there was no cure from the day it was diagnosed, and it's evident now that Ken's ministry was, as John Morton, MSIA spiritual director, put it, "on fire" right from the decision to go to Mexico. Did you know that one of the Gerson patients was a University of Santa Monica student and our interactions helped her subscribe to MSIA Discourses? Then in Texas, a first-year Discourse subscriber was wavering about renewing her second year but did so as a result of witnessing the unconditional service her Houston community shared with us. The Houston ministers had their own profound experience of loving service, including the extraordinary bonding that became evident between Babalola Chris-Rotimi and Kenny. And Kenny's sisters are also reaping the gifts of all the outpouring of love.

Not to mention our own personal iron-clad commitment to do whatever it took to take every step we could toward healing— Spirit meeting us at the point of our action daily. Ken's will to live, his recognition that he was living on Spiritual energy, and our complete and utter loving for each other sustained us both for months on end, extending his life at least several months beyond the statistics.

From all those lifetimes before, through this one and into eternity, our love remains unchanged—unconditional, overflowing, and in the oneness J-R reminds us is true. He is me and I am him and doing for him was as if I were doing for me. No words can really describe what I'm trying to say. Suffice it to say I wouldn't do it any other way. There is no other way.

—Katherine—

Oh, wonderful Carol. Thank you for writing this to Patti and for sharing it with all of us. You teach us with your passage into the Light. I weep as I read, and I am inspired to be even more loving in each moment that I continue to breathe.

I love you.

PS It also helps me to appreciate that however my soul directs me in my transitioning process, it will be an opportunity to hold the Light and to serve up until the last moments.

—Valerie Kampmeier—

Carol, thank you so much for sharing this with us. I'm moved to tears by your insight, your courage, your tender devotion to Kenny, your love for each other, and your dedication to your spiritual path. You are such an inspiration. I hope you will take precious care of yourself and reach out for support when you need it. And sleep...

Much love and Light,

Val xxx

—Janet—

Love is the most powerful energy in the world, and you two certainly had that, rest now sweet Carol, cry, heal. I promise each day gets easier, I am coming up to a month since John passed and trying to move forward. I will be in touch.

—Celia—

Carol, God bless you and thank you for sharing with us. Reading your words of love so inspired me; for they truly were words of love, of bringing God's loving here on this planet for us to experience and share with you. I am grateful.

Kenny and Carol engaged to be married
at the Island House 1995

Red-Tailed Hawk—Kenny's Spirit Symbol

Chapter 27

Dear Sisters, an Accounting of One Day in a Life

April 6, 2010

March 13, 2010. Kenny 17 days before passing into Spirit. Peace and joy!

Carol here, continuing Kenny's blog as a way to train my own consciousness to find the good in each day and share it with you. Ken's ministry near the end of his life was to share his experiences of the presence of Spirit in hopes that even just one person would benefit. I hope to continue for him in my own way.

Today I wrote to Kenny's sisters. Here's what I said:

I'm planning to go back to work in May. I have so much to do with assessing our bills, changing ownership of Kenny's car, and the various little investments we did make on paper. Clearing out our bedroom of all the clinic-type stuff, disposing of clothes and the many big and little "things" Kenny accumulated over the years. We will organize a yard sale, I have donated some to a non-profit, a friend will put some on eBay for me, and of course I will keep the most important things close to me. My friend Muriel is helping me put all that together. Not to mention taxes. I have filed for an extension through the tax guy that did ours a couple of years back. Muriel will add up my categories, and the tax guy will file for me. Thank goodness!

So when I'm immersed in paperwork and phone calls, I'm okay. It's when I stop to take a rest and realize he's not here with me, I cry. You have to understand though, I've been crying for months, ever since the diagnosis. Kenny too. He was so vulnerable, so tender, and any loving gesture from me or anyone else would make him cry and then I would cry. We mostly cried out of gratitude for every way Spirit paved the way. We understood that our experiences were precious, even though as time wore on, it was inevitable that Spirit would take him soon. We also cried knowing we didn't have much time left. One day he got a little testy with me and I with him. Then I hugged him and told him how sorry I was that I lashed out and that I wouldn't knowingly do anything that would hurt him. He cried and I cried not wanting to waste any more time on being grumpy.

Alas he did get grumpy after that from time to time, and I had to say to him and myself that I had no idea what it must have been like in his body as the cancer began to take over in very evident ways. Grumpy Kenny was then allowed in my mind, and I found myself apologizing daily for little things I could not make better for him, things like how food began to taste bad. He had very little saliva, so it all got mealy in his mouth. He'd have to sip water with every mouthful. He couldn't swallow without turning his head to the side (there was a tumor in his neck constricting his throat—I remembered seeing it on the scan). I couldn't turn him sometimes without hurting him. He sweated through all the bedclothes, and I wouldn't remember to freshen the pillow enough. The smell of the gasoline leaf blower. The noise of construction in the neighborhood, the sun in his eyes when I forgot to close the blinds in time. The enormous effort it took for him to walk, and near the end, he stayed in bed for the last two weeks. No more showers for a man who loved his precious water. He did love his bed baths though. The sometimes insensitive bath nurses. A few visitors who stole energy instead of sharing it.

In all of this were his forgiveness and his gratitude, evident to anyone who came to call. And his amazing Divine eyes that looked at me with such loving. And his forever smile. He'd fall asleep while I was wiping his face or feeding him some food, and when he'd wake up, he would giggle like he'd just committed a little faux pas.

Before the diagnosis, we had many differences that looked insurmountable. After the diagnosis, we became single-minded, heading toward the goal of making him well. All differences melted away. No more resentments, no grudges, no regrets, just one mind and one heart doing everything possible to squelch the oppressor. This is one of the most powerful things that sustained his life, along with the knowledge that in the last couple of months he was living on spiritual energy, way past when the statistics would have taken him out.

If I could have stayed awake 24/7 I would have, knowing that every second counted.

Lastly, and I know I wrote a lot more than you asked for, it helps me to do this. And I feel a calling to post these kinds of writings on Kenny's blog, to continue his ministry of sharing his experience with folks with the intention of assisting at least someone out there to get through their own trials with grace and dignity and just a glimpse of what's possible when we are aware of the presence of Spirit in our lives.

———

—Katherine —

Beloved Carol,

Thank you so much for putting all of this down on paper. It is an extraordinary reminder of how fleeting time is for each of us, especially in our relationships with loved ones, and how precious it is to let go of anything that detracts from our loving. Thank you for gifting us all.

I love you

—Valerie—

Thanks so much for continuing to write, Carol. I was so happy when I saw there was another blog entry. And of course, do what works for you. I really appreciate the honesty with which you shared about the hard times as well as the good. Your loving for each other was so evident, and yet your honesty stops me from putting you both on a pedestal in some state I can never reach. Knowing that you overcame the grumpiness moment by moment inspires me to keep doing the same. Thanks also for the beautiful photograph. Kenny's shining eyes blew my heart open every time I saw him.

Much love, Light, ease and grace to you. I am so glad you have people supporting you in practical ways, as well as through the Light.

Chapter 28

What's It like to Leave This World?

Carol, April 9, 2010

A friend who has the ability to "look in on" things and people wrote, "Ken Jones passed tonight... around 11:30 p.m., March 30. I knew from the sound of Carol's crying. So I went and stood by their door for a while holding the Light and chanting my tone along with sweet Bryce. When I looked in on him spiritually, he was ecstatic, enjoying the rapturous bliss of release with many souls and much Light around him. And he was way beyond happy... his was a magnificent graduation from this earthly level. Well done, Ken... and Godspeed."

He called what he saw "The Reception" of Kenny into the higher realms. Gacky's essence was there as he lifted up. And then the ascension took place within a golden Light. I have only heard this kind of description of death associated with Jesus. But according to what I understand of John-Roger's teachings, many of us can have the same kind of experience, especially those who know who they are in the eyes of God.

Here's a little more about Gacky, Kenny's grandfather.

Do you believe there is an afterlife or that some people can touch in to the spirits of those who have gone before us? The day before Kenny passed, he had that phone consultation with Dr. Edward Wagner, a practitioner who can see other levels of existence. Without any prior information he asked if I knew anything about Kenny's father's father. Because Kenny could only whisper the few days before he passed, I told the doc that it was Gacky and that he died of prostate cancer and that Kenny was by his side when he died.

The doc said Kenny was concerned about breaking our hearts, those of us he left behind, and that Gacky's spirit was there with Kenny to help him go in peace and beauty. Not to worry about anyone's heart or mind or soul. There's no more to heal, no negative imprints to clear, and no harm being done. Gacky is fusing his spirit to Kenny's to give him peace and the ability to let go with a sense of completion on all levels of existence.

Doc said he is very fortunate to have a soul like Gacky to help him at this time. He said Gacky told him Kenny was blessed to have Divine eyes, to have been called to God when he was very young, and to be protected from family dynamics. He said Kenny would understand everything very soon.

So I'm sharing this to help make it easier to let a dying loved one go. It's tough. From my own experience, I wanted every moment I could possibly have with Ken. I didn't want him to go. In fact, the first time he thought he would pass soon, he woke me in the middle of the night to tell me good-bye. Well, this wrenched my heart so much I began to mutter how much I loved him. His response was, "Stop trying to pull me back."

I stopped talking and just held his hand. It took about a week for him to actually come to his last hours, but what an eye opener that was. It was from that moment forward that I became as respectful of his space and timing as I possibly could. I wasn't always conscious however. Once I was whispering to one of the HeartReach team, and he told me, "Too much talking." Another time I was typing, and he told me, "Too much clicking, too long!" But mostly I was right there with him trying to anticipate his needs and be mindful of not pulling on his energy. I could only do what I knew how to do and trust that God (and Gacky) would take care of the rest.

I wrote a few days ago that Ken's last hours were difficult (in my eyes). I had expected that a peaceful death meant the person just slipped into sleep and didn't wake up. But a few hours before Kenny passed, his breathing was very labored and halting, and he moaned and thrashed about. Then after we administered enough drugs to quiet him, he breathed easy for a few minutes and then just stopped breathing.

All this was frightening to me, and I thought it might have been my fault that I didn't give him enough pain medicine. So I confessed to John Morton, who can also see through spiritual eyes, and his response was that it was all "part of the process." That Kenny was clearing up the last bit of karma before he took off into the heavens. John also told me a few days before Kenny left that I shouldn't worry about "missing the moment" when Ken would leave because I would be called to be there. That was also true. I had fallen asleep once we quieted Kenny's breathing but spontaneously woke up in time to tell him he was loved and that the Traveler was right there to take him home. With this he breathed a few more breaths and then no more.

I hope this is comforting and helpful. Nothing comforts like overcoming an illness, and I wish that for anyone. But in the face of no return to normal, productive life, with a lot of prayer, and seeing the good in all experiences, we can walk through the most challenging times trusting that God is good and everything is meant for our learning, growth and upliftment. And everything is perfectly orchestrated by our souls anyway—that's still a hard one for me to grasp. I suppose when it's my time, I will get it. I'm sure I will. I have my Kenny's amazing strength and foresight to lean on. And it'll be grand to know he'll be there for me like Gacky was for him. Now I'm excited about it, and so was he! He said so.

Bless you all.

—Judith—

Good morning, Carol,

Thank you for sharing your heart here. What a tender and blessed time it is. I'm keeping you and Ken's sweet soul in my prayers. Remember to be gentle with yourself. Grieving has a life of its own and has no regard for our plans. But somehow, through God's grace, we do move on and suddenly one day you find that the primary state of your consciousness is not the process of grieving, but the journey of redefining and living your own life with the comfort of the love and memories you carry of the tenderness you shared.

Godspeed, Kenny!

May the peace and love of God be with you, Carol!

—Joan Beisel—

Your sharing is so confirming of our work in MSIA. Kenny was a role model for me to know that all is well as I am on my way home. And Carol, you too are a role model for a minister who supported and loved beyond the physical dimensions. I will miss Kenny, but he is in my heart always.

—Esther—

Beloved Carol,

Oh how gratifying it is to have these blog entries. I just read through all of yours and now I have a clearer sense of the glory of Ken's passing. What a privilege to read these intimacies. Thank you for posting them. The last time I saw Kenny was on that funny, sweet Pie Day that he described earlier. I feel deeply honored to have been in the presence of you two in the past several months. Thank you for sharing yourselves so openly and truly.

With great loving and appreciation.

—Jim Stratigakes—

Dear Carol,

I am grateful for you and Ken. I read the interview of Ken in the New Day Herald and realized how much Ken is giving to all of us about being votaries of the Traveler and how to be with completing this life and transitioning through physical death into the Light. I am deeply touched by his Spirit, grace, and his loving humor.

Thank you for sharing via the blog. The teachings continue. I am remembering Ken sitting at the head of our dining room table when you visited Rosanne and me. I can see his big loving eyes, easy smile, and his being a "Southern Gentleman." What fun! You both moved with so much grace.

—Karen Powell—

Dearest Carol,

I loved reading your blog and reading about how you are taking good care during this time of momentous transition. Caring for yourself also cares for us, and your words shed much Light for me. I had the honor of working with "Apache Scout" [Ken's handle] on leather binding about twenty fairy-tale books I had written for my family. He did an exquisite job. These beautiful storybooks live on in my family's shelves in the US and Mexico. Thank you again, Carol. Much loving to you.

—A friend wrote—

Dearest Carol,

Thank you so much for this. What an amazing service you and Ken give to all of us. I don't think I ever met Ken in person, and I don't know you well, but here I am in Spain sobbing the deepest sobs, feeling the profound grief and gratitude.

"Concerned about breaking our hearts—those of us he left behind." Hard to read that and not choke up. Yes, that is often a part of the process I think. I once wrote about the last words my grandmother said before dying from her second heart attack at forty-seven, "I did not get to say good-bye to my babies." They were seven and twelve, and I was two and a half, yet I still carry some deep grief and gratitude inside me for her and the sudden physical disappearance... more than fifty years ago.

To hear information from those who can "look in on" the other side is so healing. So moved by the Gacky story. There seems to be such a sacredness around the time of passing. We had many miraculous things that happened when my brother passed quickly and far from anyone he knew... as if his spirit wanted to make sure we got the news that he was fine.

The transitions of birth and death have always fascinated me and also bring up great fear inside me. We are all kept so separate from both in our society. Your sharing and Ken's sharing here are such an important ministry in this greatest mystery of life.

Blessings to you in this transition! Give yourself all the time in the world to heal.

—Cynthia Collier wrote—

I was driving home to Vista from inland Encinitas, when my intuition nudged me to take the coast route. It was a paradisiacal afternoon, warm and clear, the ocean spectacularly blue. Gazing westward at its beauty, I noticed something in the sky flying north.

It looked like a bird but seemed way too big to be one. I wondered if it might be a hang glider or some kind of motorized small aircraft. I drove at a speed to stay even with it and was going about forty to fifty miles per hour, when I saw it flap its wings one time, at which point I realized it was a big pelican. A really big pelican. Fascinated, I determined to keep pace with it, amazed at how fast it was flying, wondering if it was just enjoying a strong current of air. In the meantime, large flocks of pelicans soared by, most of them going south. I've never seen so many pelicans all at once! And it seemed a little odd that this one was all by itself, going in the opposite direction. Then, suddenly this huge guy makes a big right turn and starts to fly east, until he's right next to me— maybe ten or twenty feet away—and we're still soaring up the coast, but now together very close. He definitely was tuned into me, as we flew along, and I was getting chills, and the tears started to flow.

It hit me then—is this Ken saying "Hello. I'm okay!" as he'd told you and others before his passing last March that he was going to come back (as a hawk) and let everyone know he'd made it to another realm? I looked over at him feeling this realization, and I said out loud, "Ken, is that you?" As soon as I did, he turned and headed west, toward the sea, and then north again, eventually melting into the sky...

It was an exhilarating interface with Nature and God and the mystery of life for sure... I felt shaken and honored at the same time, not clear about what had happened but knowing it was special. The fact that it was such a huge bird was one thing—king of the pelicans? I've never seen one that big before. It was incredible. And I felt very grateful, reconnected to the mystery of life big time. Maybe he decided to opt for the magnificence of a pelican just for me that day!

Chapter 29

Fourteen Days Later

Carol, April 14, 2010

A myriad of feelings, thoughts, and actions! Today at 11:24 p.m. marks two weeks since my Kenny left this world. I still cannot believe it when I actually think about it. Sometimes I think he will walk in the door any minute. When I'm out on an errand, I feel I can't wait to get back home to be with him.

Compiling picture albums for the memorial this Saturday. Cynthia, his sister, started one loaded with pictures from Kenny's childhood all the way up to our courtship. I'm finishing it with wedding pictures and many others from that day forward. A friend is also creating a beautiful montage of photos of Kenny and images he loved with captions that give a flavor of his passions and who he was (according to me anyway).

Interesting that many years ago, when our relationship was a little rocky, I looked at old pictures of him thinking he wasn't so cute in those days. But now I see every one of them in a new Light. His Spirit shined through them all—in his smile, in his eyes, in his sweetness, in his protectiveness of his sisters, in his sense of adventure and his love of nature. My, how the consciousness can sway with the times when we are looking at the lower levels. He looked at his own pictures recently and told me what a sweet boy he was. We both teared up and took the opportunity to love up the boy still peeking out through those divine eyes!

The last few days when he could hardly swallow and wasn't eating or drinking very much because everything made him hiccup and burp hard, I'd swab his mouth with little sponges on sticks soaked in water. He loved them. Called them lollypops and could he have a lollypop please, savoring each one with delight.

They say the memorial will help define a milestone. That maybe it will get easier to think about him without welling up. I dunno. Maybe. Then there will be more of them on the east coast and the ashes. I don't want to do any of this. I don't want to go through papers or figure out assets, or mount pictures or clean out clothes or sell stuff or decide what to give away. It's all so final.

Eeeek! Letting my emotions and my mind get the better of me. Time to turn to the teachings of the Spiritual Heart to comfort myself. Time to know that Spirit orchestrates everything and no one leaves without perfect timing. But it was too short. Another ten or fifteen years would have been just grand. Another month or even a day. It took a life for me to experience unconditional loving and unconditional service. What a sacrifice. Thankfully he told me many times in the last weeks of his life how happy he was. He had everything he needed, he said.

In that I find a little peace.

—

—Celia—

I am so moved every time I read your blog and loving words of dear Ken. Thank you for continuing. It's a blessing for me and I'm sure for you too.

I won't be able to attend Ken's memorial for I'll be in San Diego doing services, but I am and will continue to celebrate him in my heart. When we were in Seattle or Portland we were sharing with John and Leigh our Ken stories. I am going to pick up a copy of Kenny's wilderness teacher, Tom Brown's *Grandfather* this afternoon. When Leigh told us how much she loved it, I knew it was my next one to read. As she spoke about it I was really touched in a deep way. I'm looking forward to sharing with Ken his favorite book.

Continued blessings of grace to you, sweet lady.

And again, thank you.

Our true leaders are those who look at life in a radically different way. They know that love is the radical solution. It's radical because most of us don't approach life that way. For the most part, we approach life reactively, trying to control rather than letting go.

The answer is that out of God come all things, that God loves all of its creation, and that not one soul will be lost. This is the context for living a life without fear or worry. As you integrate these truths into yourself, you will let go and relax into the arms of the Beloved.

—John-Roger with Paul Kaye, *The Rest of Your Life*

Chapter 30

Kenny's Los Angeles Memorial Service

Carol, April 20, 2010

People ask if I feel better since the memorial service on Saturday, April 17. My days are filled with many different emotions and many tasks still incomplete, each one reminding me I no longer have my sweet husband at my side, holding me, comforting me, whispering to me, sharing tender moments with me. Nor can I extend myself to him as I did every single day every waking hour since June 22, the infamous diagnosis day.

And yes, I hear this will pass. It will get better. I'll get through this okay. Friends' words of comfort slide by me without sinking in. The only comfort is sharing experiences of him, not trying to make him fade away. Right now it feels like it will never pass. I'll always be reminded of the pain in my heart. I've got ashes in my closet, bills to reconcile, death certificates to circulate, a car to sell, things to decide where they go. Things, hundreds of things. Thousands of papers to go through. Taxes. These activities are not bad, just reminders that keep me steeped in the reality that he's gone from my physical world. What! How! No! I'll wake up and it will all be a dream. Can't I have another year or two or fifteen or twenty? We were going to grow old together. Live out in the country. Grow our own tomatoes! Tend to our own animals. Sleep in the fresh air.

Spirit would ask me to find the good in every experience, every day. In that vein, the memorial was all I hoped it would be and more. Leigh Taylor-Young's officiating was flawlessly loving, gracious, genuine, warm, and embracing—just like she is in everyday life. When she hugged me, she pressed her cheek against mine and I instantly melted in her arms. She remembered Kenny called his journey "The Grand Adventure." She referred to it during the service enough so it deeply impacted those listening.

John Morton surprised us by accompanying Leigh. She whispered to me that John would like to introduce me. In doing so, he expounded on Kenny's journey. John's blessing touched my heart with a deep, abiding understanding that not one soul will be lost, and that indeed the Traveler caught Kenny and took him up, and this consciousness will catch me and all of us the same way whether we are aware or not. And if we are brave enough to realize this and stay awake to it, when the time comes like it did for Kenny, we'll experience the real treasure of consciously leaving this world.

After sharing from many people who were touched by Kenny's loving, we sang the love song "Always" by Irving Berlin. It was an old song dear to my heart that my mother used to sing and our friends sang with us at our wedding. "I'll be loving you—always..." An added bonus was the collection from *Get Lucky*, Mark Knopfler's latest album at the time. He was by far Kenny's favorite songwriter/singer.

Thank you to everyone who came to celebrate. My heart is full of gratitude to you and to my Kenny for loving me and letting me love him so fully.

———

Kenny was an avid student of Tom Brown, famous tracker and student of "Grandfather," an Apache seer.

Of Grandfather, Tom wrote,

All too many people go through life dedicated to nothing they would die for, and to him, that was not really living at all. He had a passion for the things he quested for and in so doing had a passion for living that few others could ever know. The truth, the simple truths of life, was what Grandfather was seeking. His seeking many times would lead him to the edge of death, but it was at this edge that the most profound lessons would be learned. Many times this was the only way they could be learned.

—Tom Brown, *Grandfather*

From the back cover of *Grandfather*:

"Tom Brown, Jr. began to learn tracking and hunting at the age of eight. He has founded a renowned survival school and is also the author of bestselling wilderness guides bearing his name.

"*Grandfather* is the true story of a Native American whose tribe roamed free, far from the chaos of civilization. He lived without limits or time. His world was one of eternity. His life was one of grand simplicity, where true riches were defined in the beauty of nature, and wisdom was a remarkable integration of different philosophies, of different people, tribes, and religions. Now Tom Brown, Jr., author of *The Tracker*, shares the insights of his beloved teacher—the insights of the man he called Grandfather—that speak to the eternal spirit within is all."

—Beloved friend Nicole shared—

I realize he left the body in the night, but the next day, oh my gosh... I walked outside, looked up at the mountains and the clearest blue sky I have ever seen in LA, and felt Ken everywhere. The oneness we all are was so evident. It was like heaven extended to earth, and there was singing and celebration. It was so palpable. And the amazing thing was I felt completely healed of my own illness. I had no symptoms and the fear was gone. Totally gone. I came to a new level of understanding I had not previously experienced that soared and rang in my beingness—death was not a loss but an expansion, and we are all connected intimately through the oneness, regardless of time and space. I felt as though Ken took my fears and everything else up with him to the highest heavens of God consciousness where they were transmuted, and left me with peace. The blessing has remained since. I will always be so grateful to him and his ministry, what he so gracefully taught me in life and in death (liberation).

—Janet—

Dearest Carol,

Kenny's memorial seemed beautiful. My John's is planned for May 2. Your words speak volumes to me, and gentle tears come to me as I share your heartache. I am on week six since my husband passed (I spent more than four thousand months with him in my life), so I am treating myself like I am in intensive care and surrounding myself with friends and family. I think of you every day.

—Valerie—

It was such a beautiful and meaningful service, and every time I thought of Kenny, I was so full of joy. Thank you, Carol! And one of the most amazing things to me was how wonderful you looked. I've never seen you look better. You're an amazing woman.

———

You are chosen of great love from God, because the nature of coming to this physical level is one where graduation is at hand, where you are allowed to walk out of that which has confined you, which is really to walk into Spirit and to be liberated. And as this great interest in love comes forward into your life, it is because you are choosing back to God.

John Morton

The blessing is that you are always learning what is important for your growth and fulfillment. That is an eternal blessing by God for you and everyone. Any situation that teaches you what is important and what is not important is a blessing.

—John Morton, *You Are the Blessings*

Chapter 31

What's Important and What Is Not?

Carol, April 25, 2010

In June 2009 we went to the appointment with Kenny's primary care doctor and the grave news was metastatic malignant melanoma with only three to six months at most. To make sure it was melanoma, a liver biopsy would need to be done. But from this point on, our individual purposes became one purpose—to do everything we could to halt the onslaught of this dreaded disease.

We had many differences in our relationship, our marriage. We placed different values on money and possessions. He loved to challenge the outdoors by camping out in the bitter cold without a tent and without a sleeping bag. I like seventy-two degrees best with cool breezes—not too hot please, and certainly not too cold! He loved his many possessions, things we might need if we move out on our own, things we would certainly need if the economy collapses, fun things we would use in the wilderness, weapons for when and if riots erupted. Rocks, he loved rocks. Rope and cording, grasses to make rope from, slabs of stone. An entire room full of boxes stored under the house, under the dresser, under the bed, behind the desk, in the closets. I'm still finding surprises. I barely tolerated what seemed like pretty radical thinking, especially when it resulted in buying more things, but as I think about it now, these times he was preparing for may still befall us.

He loved western movies and TV shows, and during his treatment, watched episode after episode of Steve McQueen's *Wanted Dead or Alive*. I didn't have a love of any specific movie genre, but please, not another western! Though near the end I learned to appreciate why he loved *Appaloosa* so much and gladly watched it with him several times—he saw it thirteen times!

He virtually hated TV commercials and muted the sound for every single one of them when he held the remote. If I held the remote, I'd go unconscious and not think twice about how loud or inane it was. Little stuff like that!

Money—well that's a guarded personal matter that always presented us with challenging conversations, promises, and ultimatums that never lasted.

But we did believe in our marriage vows, and every time it looked like our differences were insurmountable, one of us would ask (dreading the answer), "Do you want a divorce?" And the other would always answer no (whew! What a relief!), and add, "But I don't want things to stay the same." We did make some progress during those years, very slow, painstaking, sometimes grueling. But we always abided by our deep love underneath it all. And yes, we had our share of little annoyances and judgments and huge differences.

But the diagnosis startled us into unconditional loving in the blink of an eye. From that day forward, all petty and big differences were put aside, shelved, disregarded, and mostly forgotten. The most important thing was discovering a therapy that he felt would work for him and embarking on it as soon as possible. As for my part, I would do whatever was necessary to support his decisions and the therapy. I knew my role, and I relaxed knowing I did not need to make decisions for him. It was his body and his treatment and his relationship with God and the Traveler.

What's important? Loving each other is important and saying so—daily. Do what you know how to do and leave all the rest to God, that's important. Ask for spiritual assistance. Know that you will receive it. Look into each other's eyes. Tell each other you'll be there to hear whatever the other has to say. Trust Spirit to show you the next step on your path. Touch each other consciously putting love into your hands. Tell your loved one what you admire about them and have tolerance for their "other" qualities. During those months of one focus, I often told Kenny he was my hero, my Miracle Man—and indeed every day he demonstrated fearlessness, strength on all levels, humor, open-heartedness, and gratitude. As his illness progressed, he would express more love, more appreciation, more generosity, more good things of the soul.

Forgiveness, saying I'm sorry for any time I hurt you or was mean to you. Reading to each other from meaningful passages in favorite books. Did I say looking in the same direction? Did I say trust in Spirit? And know that if you do your part, Spirit will match your actions with tangible support that you may very well recognize, and if you do, gratitude could fill you so completely that it could take your breath away.

What's not important (in other words, what *not* to put energy into)? The petty differences, the old judgments, the mindless chatter and worry. The history. Old broken promises. Old anything!

Make a point to learn from your differences. Each of you has gems of knowledge and wisdom. How exciting to look at those differences as a learning opportunity!

I could tell many more stories of how our love prevailed, but the bottom-line message clearly is to love, forgive, accept, understand, be grateful on a daily basis. Be with each other as if this were the last day you had together—practice what that would look like because some day it will come. Look in the same direction—one mind, one heart, one focus on spiritual fulfillment and service.

In all his days, Kenny searched for meaningful work, a career he could depend on to last. He contributed to mankind in many helpful ways through the many vocations and interests he chose to explore. The one that lasted the longest and flourished the greatest was his MSIA ministry. He was always good at sharing his experiences and teaching others all the myriad of things he learned almost daily, and this escalated such that after the diagnosis, he was an open book to anyone who cared to listen. And each day as he neared leaving this planet, he shared more of his joy, more of his love, his gratitude, and his discoveries as a child of God—his ordination blessing was obviously being expressed every day. He knew where he was going and he looked forward to it. I witnessed this steady awakening in awe, in appreciation, and in unconditional loving as much as I knew how.

Being sick and not able to do much for himself, he had many requests of me throughout the days, and I did respond physically almost 24/7. I was tired and worried and spent many hours each day juggling all his needs and at the same time keeping my own body strong. If I had it to do over again, the only thing I would do differently is not so much "clicking," as Kenny would put it. Spend less time doing things and more time just being with Kenny, touching him, bathing him, listening to him, and making him comfortable. Oh, I did plenty of all of that, but missing him so much now I want more!

Towards his last days, Kenny couldn't swallow more than a squirt of water at a time, but his mouth was always extremely dry. The nurse brought him some sponges on sticks that were to be soaked in water and used to swab his mouth. He called them lollypops. "Lollypop please." So I held his head up a bit in the right position so he could swallow the little bit of water that he squeezed out of the sponge with his teeth and swished around in his mouth. He'd say, "I love lollypops. They're so good. Water, I love water. More, more, more." And that forever smile would accompany the words. As much as holding his head and reaching for the sponges made my arms and back ache, I loved those moments when such tiny things would give him pleasure.

These last months of our life together are an imbedded experience of what's important and what's not. I pray I can carry this experience forward into the rest of my life. Right now grief wells up in me daily and I just let it come. My ministry in this moment is to tenderly offer myself the caring and love I so freely gave to Kenny.

What's important and what's not...

Oct 30, 2010, eight months after he passed

I said, "Kenny, give me a sign you are present." The sign was this inner message:

Yes, it just took your stopping fidgeting. I'm here now. I'm loving you and as usual admiring your tenacity. I love, love, love, this project [the book] and will continue to contribute my message. Death is glorious. I know you miss my physical presence but you have the rest of me whenever you tune in and if you want to feel me physically, do like you have been and imagine me spooning you.

I'll come to you in your dreams. I promise. Don't doubt me—I don't give empty promises from where I am. And when I was with you physically, I believed in those earthly promises. I didn't know I couldn't always deliver them. So going forward, here's one thing I want everyone to know and you can repeat it often:

Tell them I said I'm really here in some ways more than when I was alive on earth. I know remembering my physical presence makes you sad. But just think of what we have ahead of us—one of the most poignant gifts of our time with the Traveler's energy on it and the wisdom of the ages. See if you can tap in to one of the ancient ones. Try Isaiah for one. I love you, sweetie, you're my best of all bests. I know you're thinking about others I have loved, but while I loved them a lot, I could not give them then what I'm giving you now—which is love everlasting and the opportunity to witness conscious dying and resurrecting and a relationship that keeps on giving and growing. I'm sorry I had to leave the physical to give you all this, but it was my agreed upon time. That's all I have today, my darling one.

One of the ways we go across is faith. Prime the pump with faith.

—Janet—

Your story resonates with me. We have experienced the same journey. John and I had our challenges also, but the last year brought down any petty thoughts. We shared pure love and commitment towards his journey to the divine. He was not a believer until the bitter end. I saw his angels come in as his soul started to detach and all John kept saying was, "They are calling me." Part of my healing has been studying about the soul and our lives on earth. I am being called to your ministry, ordered your book, went to a local meeting about Eckankar. How much grief is self-inflicted on this planet. My heartache has gone from sobbing to a gentle cleansing rain as I reminisce about our thirty-five years together, and the beautiful children and homes we created together.

—Carol wrote to Janet—

Dear Janet,

My heart is with you. I find talking about my Kenny and our experiences with friends and family soothes the pain of grief. Though sometimes it does make me cry. I don't know what I would have done without the teachings of the Spiritual Heart. Our church is so solid in teaching how to love, have compassion, pray for awareness, know the highest good is taking place, trust in God, and allow one's process of awakening to unfold. I'm so glad you got John Morton's book *You Are the Blessings*. It is enlightening and comforting. You mentioned that you are drawn to our ministry, one way to steep yourself in the teachings is to subscribe to MSIA's Soul Awareness Discourses. There's a great explanation of these discourses on the MSIA website, better than I could describe here. So just log onto www.msia.org to learn more. Or just to get your feet wet, you can request the free introductory book by John-Roger called *Journey of a Soul*. Stay in touch, Janet. I'll support you in whatever way I can.

—Mary McClary—

Carol,

I have read your blogs through—thank you for sharing from the depths of your soul, so graceful, so steeped in loving all while grappling with the very human response to great loss.

May you continue to be borne on the wings of Light as you move through this process.

—Esther—

Dearest Carol,

I'm only now catching up with your blog.

My dear, you write so beautifully, so tenderly, and with great integrity of your marriage to marvelous Ken and your final days together. I feel most grateful for these glimpses into your life and journey together. Such intimate sharing, yet available to all those who wish to know. A gift to all of us.

Blessings and Light

———

I include this message as an example of Kenny's insight into my consciousness. The essence of this message is urging me to let go and come present. To let go of trying to recreate the experiences in the way I wished I would have participated and to accept myself in the spiritual perfection as I am. To accept past experiences as they were—simply because I cannot change the past. I can, if I want to, wallow in it, or use it for my upliftment, learning, and growth—another deeply essential teaching of the Spiritual Heart.

On December 5, 2011, through my hand, Kenny said:

Hey, honey—do me a favor and take the noose off your neck. You've already hung yourself many times in other lifetimes, and it's not necessary this lifetime. I love you too much not to tell you that. In fact, I caught you doing it one time and couldn't get you down in time and that set up the whole karmic dynamic of those thirty-five lifetimes when we assisted each other in dying. Clear yourself, honey!

Love you, K

Chapter 32

What Will Quell the Avalanche of Tears?

Carol, May 5, 2010

The last three days have been excruciatingly painful. I cry over just about everything. Remembering how Kenny's body lost strength, lost muscle, lost blood, and that was just what I could see with my naked eye. Every day was its own reality. Slowly each day he couldn't do something he could do the day before until I was moving his arms for him and lifting his head for him, and feeding him and wiping his face and helping him cough and breathe easier.

Today my friend Muriel came over, and for the fourth Tuesday in a row she has been helping me sort out medical bills and calculate assets, and research information. Today she spent the entire day editing a letter I feel obliged to send to the clinics that Kenny enrolled in for treatment. That made me cry out of gratitude. And when Gail and Yvonne took me out to see the Renoir exhibit at the Los Angeles County Museum of Art tonight, that made me cry.

Suddenly I will flash on "there's no return from here." We can't make up and then he'll come back to me. I won't see him walk in the door and kiss me after a day's work. I can't race back to him after doing an errand. This is permanent—after nine months of blood, sweat, and buckets of tears, there is no more. That makes me cry. I sound indulgent to myself, yet this is real. Everyone says it will get better, but I don't want my memories to fade, I don't want to forget, I don't want to feel less, and I don't want to go on. I just want to look at pictures of us, hear recordings of his voice, read his blog and his poems, and remember everything like it was yesterday so he will stay alive inside me.

Doing spiritual exercises (meditation) helps—when it helps. At least I have some relief from the pain of loss for the time I am meditating out of my body. Prayer helps—dear God, give me a new purpose. Show me in ways I will understand what it is. Give me the courage and strength to do whatever it is that you want me to do. I received a condolence card today from a friend who wrote, "Our prayers are with you as you go through this very difficult journey of recovery and enlightenment as you see where God wants you." Wow, that touched me deeply. See where God wants you.

Okay, today I will be open to seeing where God wants me. And if I learned anything during those months taking care of Kenny, I learned that God would respond to my action. It always did in palpable ways that I understood. Okay, God, I'm on notice now, please reveal where you want me. *Baruch Bashan*—the blessings already are!

I had written to John Morton, letting him know that my spiritual exercises were fraught with images of Kenny's last days and the only relief was when I fell asleep. His suggestions were

1. Do free-form writing, a technique for emptying the mind of whatever comes up. Writing out what the mind is saying in continuous stream of thought is therapeutic.
2. Get an aura balance. Aura balances are offered by MSIA as a service to anyone who would like assistance in balancing the aura, removing thought forms and clearing negativity through love, compassion, and forgiveness.

3. To be gentle with and accepting of myself during this time of healing. If self-judgments come up, I can just allow that and do self-forgiveness and place Light into myself. I don't have to focus on any judgments but can shift my focus to the Light and allow the grace of the Christ to heal it all.

—Robert—

Being honest, being present, writing about what is—all seemed to help in my own experience with grieving. Even though you may feel out of control, from my perspective you seem to be on track and really supporting yourself beautifully through this process. It's inherently messy. Be kind to yourself. You're in my heart.

—Mollie Morgan—

Dear Carol,

This blog (Kenny's and now your sharing) is an amazing blessing of service. It has touched me in so many ways, I cannot express. I am blessed for being a part of your lives.

Love and Light,
Mollie

The love of looking at a newborn baby is divine love. The look of two young lovers is divine love.

It is all divine love when we have placed the highest good of that person ahead of our actions towards them.

You know it's very hard to love in a divine way because it can't be understood with the mind. It's spiritual. This oneness with all humanity is within the heart of every being.

—John-Roger with Paul Kaye, Living the Spiritual Principles of Health and Well-Being

Chapter 33

Old Love Letters and Leather Tools

Carol, May 14, 2010

Kenny and I lived in a really big historic house with a lot of other people at Peace Awareness Labyrinth and Gardens (and MSIA headquarters), and I still live there. Underneath the first floor is a crawlspace almost tall enough for a short person like me to stand upright. Our stored stuff takes up the floor space of a twelve foot by twelve foot room. Mostly it's Kenny's "someday, maybe" projects, tools, equipment, and memorabilia from past experiences and relationships, craftsman supplies, and many different types of disaster preparedness paraphernalia. Among the boxes of papers I found love letters, good-bye letters, and letters from his family, which I pored over until one o'clock in the morning. Notably many were from his mother recounting her own bout with cancer and cancer treatment. All were from 1989 through '95. These years correspond to his sojourn in Hawaii, beloved Kauai to be exact. Photographs too—a glimpse of my husband in his younger years before we met.

After reminiscing over his previous accounts of living through Hurricane Iniki (which by the way, was harrowing) and reading all this mail, I found myself so sad for his many years of soul searching and break-ups and the deaths of a younger sister many years ago and both his parents within the last fourteen years. And the last nine months of his life and all the choices we made to try to help, and how the melanoma, first lurking in the background, made itself more intrusive month by month, then week by week and finally each day it was, as he put it, "Taking me out."

There's only so much of poring over and deciding over each little and big thing he left behind that I can do before I get emotional again. It's all okay, crying is okay, remembering is okay, and picturing is okay, except for the imagination going haywire on negative images. Then I have to call a halt, call in the Light and do something different to switch the energy. I'm about one-fourth of the way through it all, having already labeled some boxes "eBay," some "Yard Sale," "Resale Store," and "Throw Away." The little things I'm keeping include the beautiful bow he carved out of Osage orange wood, and the shell necklace from our tenth anniversary Kauai vacation. Before the yard sale opens to the public, I will call his Tom Brown tracker friends to come preview and pick out what they want. I know he would really love that.

Still hovering over hospital and doctor bills, waiting for insurance to play their hand, and still clearing his iPhone in order to give it away. Do you know how many thousands of details make up a life? I don't either, but it's been nearly six weeks since he passed, and I've only touched a small fraction of his belongings. It's not so much the work involved. It's more the emotions involved. The way some things bring up memories of the hard times when we didn't see eye to eye. When our differences and our hard-shelled camps separated us. When I withheld love because I was so angry. When I couldn't help but fall into family patterns of "disapproving" of his actions because they were my patterns as well. When with great relief I could admit that to myself and to him, it began to change, and I began to have more compassion for his roots and the patterns that resulted. When I could climb out of myself to put myself in his shoes. I had small experiences of these awarenesses as our relationship matured, but it wasn't until the diagnosis that I fully surrendered to the fulfillment of my ministry to my husband. The surrender indeed was sweet, and it got sweeter throughout the months of caring for him, but the lesson was hard-won, my friends.

Don't wait until one of you has a terminal condition to put yourself in each other's shoes. Miracles of unconditional love await you. The timing gets perfect. The circumstances start looking like the best they can be given the situation. The Spirit becomes palpable and the prayer is ongoing, 24/7. As if it were the last prayer you'll ever utter. Spirit responds to sincerity and genuine asking. Seek Spirit and honor it in each other, as John-Roger says, "like you would seek your next breath." We had nine months together once we surrendered to the loving, and it was all too short. I'd have given him some of my years if I could.

This comes out of deep loving for the process that unfolded in my life and deepest gratitude to my Kenny for his sacrifice in my journey back to the heart of God. God bless us all.

—Janet—

Embrace the memories. Take one hour at a time, one task at a time. Each day is a little easier. Do not put pressure on yourself to move through this process. Every time I step outside, a little butterfly comes and sits with me. Yesterday the butterfly's wings were a bit chewed up, which made sense to me. We both know despite all efforts it was their time. I am starting to believe cancer starts in your thoughts, as John had very low self-esteem all his life, even though he was the best father and artisan that I knew. His life lessons were too late. I think you and I have a lot to share with anyone who wants or needs to listen, and somehow I think this is the path I am supposed to take in the future when I sort through this mess. Your words are very helpful to me as I am experiencing the same feelings and feel very overwhelmed with a half-finished house and a garage full of tools and stuff! The company of my children and friends keeps me moving forward. God bless you. Carol.

—Carol replied—

Dear Janet,

God bless you too. I hope you find comfort in your family. My birth family and my spiritual family are wonderful people, ready to support me in whatever way I need. I am truly blessed. And I know you are too.

—Christine Sherwood—

Thank you, Carol, so much for sharing at such a deep, vulnerable level. Unconditional loving is a huge learning I still reach for with my family... me learning to love them unconditionally, and also expanding into loving myself unconditionally. I still fall short. You have demonstrated with Kenny, and are still demonstrating to me how it is done... what that looks like. Thank you so much for this, and God bless you as you continue on your journey.

Much love and gratitude to you,

Carol.

Chapter 34

How Spirit Works, and How Fear Can Lead to Hiding

Carol, June 5, 2010

It's been quite a while since I last posted an entry. Been working for the last three weeks, and that daily activity takes my mind away from my sorrow and my loss. One of the pleasures of my work is getting my hands into the garden here at Peace Awareness Labyrinth and Gardens. I love the gardens, the shapes and colors of the gardens, the living, loving, alive things and how they change and take shape. In doing things I love to do, I use up some mental and emotional energy in the loving. Oh, a friend told me yesterday that when she realizes she's sad over the loss of a loved one, she immediately sends that soul her loving—and as Spirit would have it, the loving comes right back to her in ways she consciously experiences. Isn't that wonderful? I'm going to try it myself.

I've also continued the task of unboxing Kenny's boxed-up things upon things and deciding where they go. The task of notifying a myriad of businesses, associations, and contacts that Ken had died. The task of communicating with hospitals, doctors, and insurance companies. But the most important message today is about how Spirit works. My friend Richard came to me a couple of weeks ago and told me that the night Ken died, he and his wife, Kate, were overwhelmed with the joy and welcoming they sensed Ken was receiving as his soul left his body. They each had their own experience of this without conferring with each other until afterward. It was as if they themselves were present on the realms of Spirit where these welcomes take place. If I understand the teachings of the Spiritual Heart, some part of their consciousness (their own souls) was present on those realms and they were conscious of it just as Ken was conscious of his soul throughout the last few months of his life here on earth.

Remember I told you about my other minister friend who had the same experience as he prayed outside our door the night Ken died? And remember I told you about how my practitioner friend helped Ken realize that his grandfather's soul was present to support his transition? And how John Morton, the spiritual director of MSIA, told me not to worry about missing the moment Ken would leave his body, that I would be called, and I *was* called out of sleep to awaken just minutes before he stopped breathing?

So when I am conscious enough to move my awareness to the Spirit that resides in me, I am comforted, I am hopeful that my future has purpose and even more loving than I've ever experienced before, and I know my birth family and my spiritual family love me and help take care of me by praying for me, by giving me space to do those tasks, and by asking if I need anything, and helping me dig into the boxes, and listen to me tell the stories I have written about here, and look at the photo album of his life, and make DVDs of the memorial service and our wedding, and CDs of our ordinations and the interview in the *New Day Herald*.

In a couple of weeks I'm traveling to the East Coast where his family will hold two more memorials for Kenny. With me I take a bunch of memorabilia and his ashes. Impersonal yet a daily occurrence on any airline on any given day. Cremated human remains, TSA calls it, and there's a death certificate to prove the box contains these remains. Deeply moving how such a common thing can be so profound when it's someone as close as a husband with whom one has spent nearly every day for years upon years. I still think he will walk in the door any moment.

My sweet and darling husband was no saint, at least not until the last couple of months of his life, and oh—now I'm remembering—not even then. He left with some secrets that I'm only now beginning to understand. In the big scheme of things, not terrible things, but what is important is that my fears fed the part of him that was compelled to hide. I was very outspoken about what I feared and that made him hide what I feared more. I know this sounds vague so I'll try to be more specific—just as a way to get clear enough for me to let go of the fears and for you to understand how fears could tempt one to hide.

I am highly sensitive to cigarette smoke. I avoid it wherever I go and choke up immediately if I smell it. Ken continued to smoke about for or five cigarettes a day throughout our marriage on the sneak. Never in my presence and always on breaks at work or in the car with the windows wide open. I never found out he still smoked after telling me he had quit years ago until he was diagnosed with stage IV melanoma. And that's when he really quit. I was shocked, but oddly enough I wasn't surprised because he knew how to hide so well. And when he or it was found out, he didn't seem to mind taking the consequences—his nearest and dearest being mad as a bat, withholding love and unable to communicate. Somehow my inability to have any altitude in these situations fit perfectly into his pattern of being scolded for things he did out of his own compulsions. This is only one example of many that showed me two people could play into each other's negative patterns just by being who they are, human beings with foibles and weaknesses.

To this day I still don't know the dynamic of Kenny's childhood that created his ability to hide. I do know the dynamic in my childhood that produced fears—doing things that my parents would disapprove of, that would create reasons to punish me, that reflected in my mother's eyes as she glared at me ready to pounce. Like flashlights under the covers at night. Like shaving my legs, and wrestling with boys. Waiting to do the dinner dishes until my grandma got up to do them. Wearing my skirts too short. And necking! Crazy, isn't it? Still, together Kenny and I created our own brand of miasma that was hard to crack. It began to disintegrate only when I realized what we were doing. Naming it started its downfall. Thank God because it freed me up enough to give my life over to serving Kenny in his hour of greatest need. I am blessed. I am grateful, I am willing to serve as my life's work. I pray for my Kenny's soul and ask him to watch over me in my elder years as I do my best to demonstrate who I have become as a result of our relationship.

In this my love reaches out to you to brighten your awareness of your own divinity. God bless you.

———

—Esther—

Dear, dear Carol,

Once again your openness and clarity move me, astonish me almost. Especially because they are crowned with—not contrition, not guilt, not self-judgment—but with that wondrous unconditional loving for self and others that I saw you and Ken demonstrate in the last months of his life. I learned so much from you both. And that learning is continuing through reading your posts. Thank you sincerely.

—Janet—

They say when you pass you go into a cocoon for rest. The other morning this big moth with blue spots came and sat with me for hours in the morning sunshine. I believe John transformed and sat with me. That is my story and I am sticking to it.

Chapter 35

The Funeral Train Began in Springfield...

Carol, June 23, 2010

They were very kind to me at airport security. I reported I had both a death certificate and "human remains" that I was carrying onboard. I also had some homeopathic medicines that could not go through the X-ray machine—incidental and ordinary compared to my never, ever in my life having carried a person's ashes on a plane after they had been stored in my closet for six weeks, hidden away from sight where I wouldn't be reminded of what they really were.

When I showed the box to the TSA officer, I was escorted to a special area. He read the label: "Certified to be the remains of Kenneth H. Jones, died on 3/30/10 and cremated on 4/13/10." He took no further steps to examine the box and didn't require me to give him the death certificate. He just wished me well and sent me on my way. The rules say you must carry human remains onboard; you cannot stow them in your checked bags. Well, this made my carry-on bag so heavy I could not lift it to the compartment above my seat. Some nice person helped me both outgoing and landing.

Just like Lincoln's funeral train bearing the president's body from town to town, we bore Kenny's ashes and picture albums, letters from and to Kenny's parents and sisters, memorabilia from their beloved Island House, and a gallon of tears from Los Angeles to Basking Ridge to Bay Head, to West Point Island where the ashes were finally released into Barnegat Bay. We were to make many stops so friends, admirers, and his family and mine could hear the stories, look at his history in pictures, say their own prayers, and celebrate his life and how much he was loved by so many.

Ken's sister Genia met me at baggage claim and took me to her house, where I spent the night. The next day we drove to her summer home on the Jersey shore, where her two sisters and their families had already been resting and preparing for the memorial, which would be just one day later. We were going to set sail on the family's beloved sneak-box sailboat, called the *Frisky*, spread his ashes out over the bay and head back to the yacht club, where we would gather to go back to Genia's house for stories, good food, and more stories and more good food.

There was no wind that morning when we woke. This could be a problem with four women in a little fifteen-foot flat-bottomed sailboat. By the time we reached the yacht club and Genia gathered us under the flagpole and Gordon delivered the poignant poem about how "I am not here, don't mourn my body," the wind had kicked up a bit. This was good news. However, in the time it took us to walk out to the very end of the dock where the *Frisky* was tied, the wind was all but howling. We got in the boat anyway and stowed the box of ashes under the stern. My job was to sit tight with my life vest on and only do exactly what I was told to do by any of Kenny's three lovely sisters, who were the *Frisky*'s crew.

Trouble brewed when we backed out of the slip and almost capsized. With a couple of swift moves, the girls had righted us and corrected a little too much, causing gallons of water to rush over the side into the boat. Genia exclaimed, "We're not going to make it!" With another maneuver the boat sideswiped another boat, whose motor had been lifted out of the water, in such a way that it dragged across the *Frisky*'s newly refinished deck and made a giant gash in the varnished surface. At this point, it was all we could do to point the boat back into the slip and get ourselves and the box of ashes off the *Frisky* and onto dry land again. As we each were given a hand or two to hoist ourselves onto the dock, dear and sweet longtime neighbor Sal Toucci offered his dock—why don't we release the ashes from there?

Here comes the rub. No one in the family wanted to go anywhere near what had been their beloved Island House property (next to dear and sweet longtime neighbor Sal Toucci's dock). After being in the family for seventy-five years, the place where the entire Jones/Newman family spent every summer of their lives, the house had been sold in 2006 and demolished by the new owners to make way for a giant summer home that spanned both lots from side to side and almost back to front. But we knew releasing Kenny's ashes from Sal Toucci's dock was the closest to Kenny's wishes we could come. He had wanted his ashes spread over the bay behind the Island House—an impossibility—but Sal's was entirely doable. We laughed and sensed that Kenny was orchestrating the whole day to come as close to the outcome he wanted as possible.

His sisters and I walked out to the end of the dock, sat down, and began taking the box out of the hand-woven bag in which I was carrying it. But the bag, having gotten wet, was now shrinking around the box, making it really difficult to handle. We managed to free the box, but I just couldn't open it. I began to cry. I asked if we could say a few words before letting the ashes go—seemed so unceremonious to just pour them out into the water.

Debbie began reciting the Twenty-Third Psalm. "The Lord is my shepherd; I shall not want…" This tender and plaintive prayer to God, this exclamation of peace and love and acceptance and knowing God's presence and protection, made me hold on to the box even more tightly and sob even more loudly. I could hear us all breaking. I felt their hands on my back. I was comforted by their presence, knowing we all missed him and loved him and laughed with him and were carrying out his wishes whether we'd planned to or not.

Finally I opened the box, and there was yet another step inside—to cut open the tie that held the inner plastic bag shut. Bill came close with his pocketknife to cut the tie, and we held the bag close to the water and let the ashes go downwind. Surprisingly they instantly dissolved into the water.

Somehow this was meaningful to me. They disappeared in a flash, just like his last breath.

We all took a moment to walk over to the new house and admire it. Sal said they were nice people, only there from June to September—nice people. So Kenny's plan not only honored their once-beloved Island House, but it also included making some kind of peace with it being gone and a new era opening up for family and friends in ways yet to be revealed. And this stop on the funeral train was complete. It was time to move on to the celebration.

~

Family friend and chaplain who would officiate over Kenny's Pickens memorial

> Thank you, Carol, for this beautiful and true story. I look forward to being part of the final stop in Pickens, where we will also have a celebration. I am thankful to have met you face to face and look forward to reading more of your writing. I think you definitely have a book going. You and Ken will finish it together! Love, Pat.

—Gail—

> My dearest Carol, you shine as brightly as our beloved boy does. The Light pours through all of your sharing on this blog, and I find myself praying for Spirit (and

your point of action) to assist you in opening the door wider, for so many others who want—(that universal truth and loving that flow from and through you) to also touch the same; to learn to believe the sweetness in themselves—in reassurance, in loving validation to their own connectedness to our never-ending flow of Source.

Or, to say it differently—I want a book out of this! I want to own a physically tangible, simple, lovely book out of this, and to share it with all those whom I touch— and I want this book for all of us, to share with all the others of us, so all of us that want this loving at this time, can find it and have it, and give it.

Your way of speaking is so genuine, well spoken, and wise... souls of many will respond, along with and through their Higher Selves... and all of us will have more opportunity to learn our own stories of loving.

What could be better! Stay your course, my friend, and keep partnering with Spirit...

Much love, oodles of gratitude—and the loving will absolutely always remain alive and well, full of *"Kenny-isms"* and *"Carol-isms"*!

Chapter 36

Finding the Inspiration to Write Again

Carol, July 11, 2010

Finding the inspiration to write this post has been difficult. I treasure every moment of my trek to Kenny's family to steep myself in our memories of him every day for twelve days straight. I felt bathed in love, compassion, understanding, and peace throughout the days, yet my writing feels stilted and not very forthcoming. But today I received a call from Janet. Janet brought her husband John to the Baja Nutri Care Gerson clinic last November while Kenny and I were there. Dear John passed into Spirit in May. I was saddened to hear this, and my heart went out to Janet. She had been reading the blog and commenting on it, but today I heard from her by phone for the first time. I heard her say the words I have said to so many. I heard myself try to comfort her, but all I could really do was understand. Even though we welcome friends and family sharing with us, no matter what profound, or caring things anyone says to us, there is still the vacuum, the broken heart, the void, the missing our dearest, closest friend in the world. The last person we said good night to and the first person we greeted in the morning. The one whose warmth kept our feet toasty at night, whom we knew was there throughout the night even if we weren't touching.

I want to tell you about my journey to honor Kenny because I knew it to be a deep and profound homage to a man who was loved by so many family and friends. Let me remind you, I'm still reading letters dating back to the 1970s, '80s and '90s and culling old bank documents, the sale of a house, and medical records, selecting which of hundreds of photographs taken through the decades to keep and which to toss. I'm being very selective, only keeping the photos without the old girlfriends. Oh, make no mistake, I had stored my own share of photos with boyfriends and "old" husbands, so I see no fault here, just noticing how my mind works.

We all come to each decade and each relationship with patterns and habits and "baggage" from the past that weigh us down. And we all hope and pray we can either hide it or dissolve it instantly, but alas, it raises its head regularly and most especially with our closest loved ones. That's the nature of how we learn in this life, on this planet, with the agreements we made about what we wanted to learn in this lifetime. Kenny had his share and we all knew it, yet his "true self" beckoned us to love him for all the sweetness and kindness, the generosity of heart, the sense of humor, the deep-blue eyes and forever smile, the constant forgiveness, the always-making-things-better side of him, and most importantly, what we all are heir to, and that is to be loved just the way we are with all our foibles and shortcomings, all our strengths and all our beingness. How many people do we know who have died and were given three memorials? Whose family traveled across country and up and down the east coast to be with each other as they honored their fallen uncle/brother/husband? If there was any part of him that didn't know his true worth in life on this planet, his soul is getting to experience it now. Oh and I can attest that in his last months, weeks, and days, he caught many glimpses of the brilliance of his own soul until he was living in that awareness consciously and daily. The shortcomings melted away, the second guessing, the hiding—they all took a backseat to what he called "A walk in the park."

I think I'm ready now to account for those incredible two weeks with the family.

———

—Valerie—

> Thanks so much for coming back to share with us, Carol. I love the end of your post particularly. May we all come to know the brilliance of our own souls sooner rather than later!

Chapter 37

The Funeral Train Stops at Chesapeake and on to Pickens

Carol, July 17, 2010

Kenny on the Island House dock, circa 2006

Cynthia, Debbie, Kenny, and Genia

All three of Kenny's sisters are amazing women. I got to spend really lovely time with each of them. After the New Jersey celebration, I visited with my dear cousins for a couple of days. I cherished that time of catching up with them, showing them my Kenny's Life Album, and sharing stories. Then it was Genia who drove me all the way from Basking Ridge to Chesapeake, Virginia, where I met for the first time the chaplain who would officiate at the Pickens memorial, and her husband.

I am reminded of what our end-of-life spiritual advisor wrote to Kenny throughout the last couple months of his life. She offered tender and moving hints about the process of letting go of the body and leaving loved ones and joining loved ones, letting us both know that symbols are important and knowing the soul never dies and is always available is important. Kenny chose the magnificent red-tailed hawk as his symbol. He's also messed with the TV a couple of times, made his portrait fall to the floor without breaking the glass, and remember best of all how he (and I'm sure God had a hand in it) changed the course of dispersing his ashes. You can read our advisor's comments throughout this book if you'd like to get a glimpse of how compassionate and attuned this lovely woman is.

Anyway, back to the events. We spent the night at the chaplain's home. She had made some delicious sangria for us and printed out the program that the family created, outlining the coming memorial service at the Pickens County Airport (I'll talk more about that later). On the front cover was one of my favorite portraits of Kenny taken at the Island House, his blue shirt emphasizing his amazingly deep-blue eyes, Barnegat Bay in the background, and a soft breeze brushing through his hair. That's the portrait at the beginning of this chapter. Sangria in one hand and tissues in the other, I couldn't help but sink into the couch sobbing yet again.

The next morning I woke up with a throbbing headache, suddenly I remembered the effects of sangria from years ago. It goes down very smoothly and I hadn't had any for so long, I forgot how it packs a wallop the next day. Genia and I tumbled into the car and headed for South Carolina—all the while Genia is driving. And all the while telling me family stories and listening to my family stories and sharing memories of Kenny. Me, I'm feeling very well taken care of in all ways. I get the sense that the entire twelve days is designed for the most grace and ease for everyone or maybe just me, I'm not sure which because it was so seamless.

That's the work of three loving and creative sisters, their husbands and kids, putting their organizational skills to work, not to mention their loving and caring and various technical skills. And I experienced every activity as a celebration and honoring of Kenny. We arrived at Debbie and John's and there had been some nice improvements to their house and land since we were there last. They built a "bonus room" where there once was a porch and garage, a great addition for big family gatherings. Plus the lake was up again which means the drought that previously had made their little cove into mud had passed and their boat was afloat again. I put my things in the sweet bedroom Kenny and I shared the last time we visited, and a pang of sadness wafted over me.

Kenny at the beach near the Jones family Island House

Two more days until the Pickens memorial. I was marking the time because I thought perhaps when this third memorial was over, I would feel different. Or at least it would represent some kind of milestone in my thoughts. I was looking forward to it for that reason and I was *not* looking forward to it for that reason. Maybe it's because I take comfort in my memories, in talking about Kenny. In reading and writing about him, and hearing others tell about him. It's almost like he's just in the other room or just down the block playing with the kids, or just out tracking a deer, getting some sun, and he will walk in the door any minute now. Then I have the sudden, (always) shocking realization that he's never going to walk in the door again and I melt into my sadness and longing. It's pretty complicated, this grief process. And I don't much like being labeled as going through "the grief process." Sounds so like an everyday occurrence, which it is in the big scheme of things. But for me it was and still is the most personal, the most undeniable and the most irreversible loss I have ever experienced.

Friday night brings us all together at Villa Novella, John III, and Casey's Italian trattoria in Central, South Carolina. Great food, lovingly prepared by nephew Chef John, served by their attentive staff and shared by all of us—sisters, brothers-in-law, nieces and nephews, cousins, me, and little toddler, Jones, the newest and darling member of the clan. We lift our glasses in a toast to our Kenny and to all of us, and tomorrow is the final memorial.

We drive to Pickens County Airport and walk into the administration building, which is dedicated to Herbert E. Jones, Kenny's father. Daddy, as he is affectionately still referred to, passed into Spirit in 2005 on his birthday—I know he is still missed. He was instrumental in building the airport and in finding funds to make improvements—highly esteemed in Pickens. So this seemed a perfectly fitting venue for Kenny's memorial service. Now comes the fun part, the actual service was to take place in the "big" hangar. Inside this really big hangar, along with a lot of open space, is a two-seater plane and a helicopter. The open hangar doors are as wide as one whole wall, and that measures I venture to say about one hundred feet across. Out on the tarmac are little planes taxiing to take off and others landing, and far into the distance are the tail end hills of the South Carolina mountains. Lush, green, and rolling under the bluest sky with tufts of white clouds meandering around and hawks circling like arrowheads. Some of us notice the hawks and acknowledge that Kenny's spirit must be present.

We prepare the space, and as I'm cutting the lemon pound cake (in preparation for the refreshments portion of the gathering), I am reminded that Kenny loved pound cake and I shed a few more tears. A hand on my shoulder and the chaplain says, "You can do this. It's okay." And I do.

She opens the service with a prayer, and then we all join in singing "Morning Has Broken" by Cat Stevens. We also recite Psalm 23. Each part of this reading touches me deeply because it is the very psalm Kenny's sister Debbie recited when we let Kenny's ashes go into Barnegat Bay.

> *The Lord is my shepherd, I shall not want.*
> *He maketh me to lie down in green pastures, he leadeth*
> *me beside the still waters.*
> *He restoreth my soul, he leadeth me in the paths of*
> *righteousness for his name's sake.*
> *Yea, though I walk through the valley of the shadow of death,*
> *I will fear no evil; for thou art with me.*
> *Thy rod and thy staff they comfort me.*
> *Thou preparest a table before me*
> *in the presence of mine enemies,*
> *Thou anointest my head with oil, my cup runneth over.*
> *Surely goodness and mercy*
> *shall follow me all the days of my life,*
> *and I will dwell in the house of the Lord forever.*

Genia and Bill's daughter, Hilary, recites a reading called "Death Is Nothing at All" by Henry Scott Holland. Debbie and John's son, John III, leads us in the Psalm of Assurance, and Cynthia and Jim's son, Tom Griffith, shares the reading called "Gone from My Sight" by Henry van Dyke. I'm reminded of meeting all these young adults as little kids fourteen years ago during my first vacation at the Island House. Mimi, as the kids called their grandmother, was still with us then, though she did pass a month later. I'm grateful to have met her.

Kenny with nieces and nephews, Tom,
John, Hilary, Karen, and Chris

Then we all sang "On Eagle's Wings" by Michael Joncas. The formal part of the service ends with the Prayer of Commendation:

> Oh God, we give thanks for our beloved brother, husband, and friend, Kenny, that You created him exactly as he was, to share our earthly pilgrimage with us. And now to You who created him, into Your arms we commend Kenny to Your tender mercy and eternal care with sure and certain hope of resurrection and his ongoing loving Spirit remaining with us, now and always.

And finally we sing "Live Forever" by Billy Joe Shaver. All the while, each presenter is backwashed in the light of the warm sunny day in the foothills of South Carolina. Chef John's delicious refreshments commenced and then I was the first to share memories of Kenny. My first message was from

Kenny—I didn't say he had delivered it after he died. But he wanted everyone to know that death is not to be feared, he said, "It's a walk in the park." And as I've shared several times throughout this book, he was a big proponent of having fun. He told me he wanted folks to have fun and if it wasn't fun, to make it fun.

Lastly and profoundly, he said, *I will keep breathing as long as Spirit gives me breath. And if melanoma absolutely must claim my body, it can have it. Melanoma cannot go where I go, because I go into the pure Spirit of the Soul Realm that is my true home.*

And we discovered through our own experience during the last few months of his life that Spirit (God) really does meet us at the point of our action. Which means we prayed fervently, we did everything we could, and we watched for the miracles to happen for the highest good of all concerned. And they did, every day.

He said he prayed for some extension of his life in order to share his story and he was given that extension based on the following promises: to be of service, to use everything for his learning, growth, and the liberation of his soul, to take care of his "sweetie wife" and to have fun. And to my knowledge, he fulfilled all those promises.

Finally, friends and family shared. Sister, Cynthia, Jimmie, Ben, and Billy, to name a few, and Genia closed the service by thanking everyone for coming out that day to celebrate.

My visit to the family is drawing to a close. We all rest the next day, take a boat ride on the lake, and watch the younger generation dive off the boat. All the while, the World Cup soccer games and some local baseball games on TV take up some idle time. Bill and Genia trek off to New Jersey on Sunday—a very long day of travel. Cynthia, Tom, and I visit Aunt Mary, where Kevin's mom and dad come to meet us. Then a short jaunt of two hours to Charlotte, where they live and where Jim has already driven Chris home from a special training at college. I've said my good-byes to each as they leave and as we leave, and I well up with yet another piece of the great loss. It's a delight to spend time with Tom and Chris—each shares their love with me in their own way.

Monday morning I wake up to Velvet's sweet eyes and cold nose. And there's time to share more stories. Cynthia tells me a side-splitting one about Genia's nail-polish remover (I won't go into detail). Jim shares his own experience of Kenny's passing, and I get to share again about how the last year with Kenny was *the* most powerful experience I have ever had of giving my life in service, of unconditional loving, of emotional intensity the likes of which are indescribable, and of his determination, strength, and oneness with all that is. I say good-bye to the boys, breaking again. And again good-bye to Cynthia and Jim at the airport. Just as I arrived alone, I leave alone, remembering that Kenny would have liked the window seat just once.

My flights back to LA were fraught with mechanical problems and endless delays, but I finally arrived back home to start the next leg of this incredible journey. The yard sale in a month and taxes two weeks later. Then maybe that whirlwind of activity that represents the diagnosis, the illness, the death, the closing of a life and all the details that go with that will subside. One thing I do know is that my darling husband lives inside me through all my tears and all my grief and all my activity and all my sweet memories. And just like every action while he was alive, I just keep doing what needs to be done out of devotion and well simply because I can.

Carol and Kenny on the Island House Dock.

Kenny would love for as many people as possible to read his account of spiritual awakening. And if my writings can be helpful to someone out there who is assisting a loved one to die gracefully, I would indeed be grateful.

———

—Cousin Jamie Cowan—

Dear Carol,

As always, I read your lines with much emotion (and not a few tears) but so impressed with your way of expressing so well the most tender and crucial parts of the story of the last days of Kenny's life and these many days since he passed on. You have done us all a great service, and I will be happy to try and pass it on to those I may come across in similar circumstances. Bless you and thank you, sweetie!

—Sharon Mill Slayback Palestri—

Dear Carol,

I saw an old friend of mine and Kenny's, Gordon Hesse, at the shore a couple weeks ago. It had been many years since we last were in touch. I was shocked and saddened when he told me of Kenny's illness and passing. Gordon was kind enough to share with me some of Kenny's final letters to him, pictures from the memorial service in Lavallette, and Kenny's blog.

The last time I saw Kenny was the first time I met you. It was the summer that the family was gathered at the Island House for the last time with Mrs. Jones, as she prepared for her next journey. It was wonderful to participate in the tremendous love in that house. That was fourteen years ago... hard to believe. Thank you for sharing so much in your writing on Kenny's blog. I felt I was a participant in something important... the completion of a life well lived by a man well loved.

Forty years have passed since I first met Kenny and his wonderful family. I am a believer that love is eternal. I spent only a short time with Kenny, but will always love him. Your love for him was palpable in your writing. I pray that that love gives you strength, joy and peace as you continue your journey. Kenny's spirit lives on in the lives of all those who knew him. I pray you find comfort in the familiar things you shared and that the memories bring a smile to your face. Fondly, Sharon

October 16, 2010, Kenny said through my hand:

Honey, understand that I am always with you and I cherish our contact. I love, love, love that you got the yard sale blog published. You did that project with such grace and brought me such dignity and respect. I love that about you. I will assist you in going forward with the book—it might take a different form. Just go with your intuition, which has been priceless so far. I will tell you when you're heading off and on. No worries. Redo my entries—it's okay. And add in the transmissions through Ruthie and certainly keep contact with Saivahni. She will be able to see where I am and help you touch in to me even more deeply. You are my beloved soul mate wife, and I treasure your soul and thank you for the depth of your love, your devotion, and your ministry to me. I carry that experience as a highlight of my existences— you are a true queen to my king, my prince, and my peon. I love you dearest, sweetie darling. Signing off, your devoted husband soul mate in God.

Chapter 38

The Ken Jones Honorary Yard Sale, Taxes, and Apache Lore

Carol, September 18, 2010

No less than one hundred boxes of Kenny's treasures were hauled out of the space under the house in preparation for the yard sale of the century (in my world anyway). A man collects a lot of things in a lifetime, especially if his interests translate to passions—passion about the Apaches; about survival in the wilderness; about survival in the city should a disaster befall us; about making books and making bows and arrows; making buckskin clothing; making camping gear like tents and quilts, gloves, hats, and moccasins; making lots of other kinds of things. Tools for the house; tools for the car; tools for all the things he made. Protective gear in case of chemical contamination; woolen overalls; waxed canvas pants; jacket; and hat. Rations in case of a prolonged disaster. Too many pairs of dress pants; outdoor pants that wore like iron; outdoor shirts that protect against the sun; suit coats; gloves, belts, hats. Books—books on birding, ducks, deer, moose, guns, and all the paraphernalia that goes with guns; Ralph Waldo Emerson biographies; nature, wilderness; tracking four-footed animals, tracking people, tracking birds, and tracking just about anything that breathes. Making movies; writing screenplays; writing poetry; children's narratives; flint knapping; and did I say guns? Art history; history of firearms;

American history; history of Native Americans; Lewis and Clarke history. Chief Joseph and his retreat to Canada. Jones genealogy; the many books by Marshall Mcluhan and Tom Brown. Ansel Adams and other photographers; Ken's own experiments as a graduate student majoring in photography and his professional work. The list is endless.

At one point as we were setting up, Bill, who was manning the sale with me, saw me tearing up over something—it almost didn't matter what it was; I can't remember now anyway. He held me while I cried. It was very comforting. Since Kenny's death, I have become two people. One goes to work and concentrates on work matters while the other comes home and takes care of the business of wrapping up my husband's life here on earth. I'm either preparing for the yard sale or doing the endless task of preparing for taxes, or looking at pictures and listening to his favorite music, or talking about him with my friends. I have many friends who in their infinite love and patience would listen until I can't talk anymore. They are very good to me.

So I purposely arranged a pre-sale day for friends of Kenny's who love all the things he loved. Four of them came all due to Kenny's friend Tracker Rob's persistent invitations. It was a very tender day as they marveled at Kenny's collection. I gave Rob some bows and arrows, a bow-stringing jig, and a bow-string thrust guide that Kenny carved by hand out of rosewood. It was an exquisite piece of art, and I would have kept it myself except I have the beautiful bow he made out of Osage orange, which is equally as artful, and I can only keep so many things. My bedroom surrounds me in photographs and things that remind me I no longer share this sweet and intimate space with my life partner.

Little did I know his life with me would be so short. Little was I willing to look at in the fourteen years we were together, but that's another story. I have a good twenty or thirty years left here on this earth. I would have liked to spend most of it if not all of it with Kenny. But instead I now attend grief recovery groups and listen to how so many people loved so many people the same as I loved my husband. What a plan this experience on earth! All for the good I'm sure, though not so evident on a daily basis. It takes strength and willingness to pull out of the loss to experience the good when a spouse or any loved one dies. I can still shock myself when I come around to realizing after the umpteenth time that he really is no longer here with me in this physical life.

I can make up stuff about how I sense his presence or know we will meet again or have faith that everything is perfect, even his leaving with unresolved karmic patterns both his and mine. But the truth is I'm not that aware of the spiritual realms right now. Meditation is fraught with images and sounds of his illness and what his magnificent body went through. And my mind wants to decide I could have made a difference if I only had more courage.

All that said, I know I just need to be reminded of my spiritual heritage, and that consciously raising my own vibration honors all he is/was when he was alive in his body and now as his soul does its work on other realms.

See that thing about his soul—I'm going on faith here because if I must make up something, it'd be great to win in my own fantasies.

Enough for now. More later about the brilliant army of spiritual warriors that surrounded us and continue to give of their extraordinary generosity. I do know from my own precious experience that adopting gratitude opens my heart and becomes the gateway for goodness to flood through.

Bless us all.

———

October 17, 2010, more from Kenny

Carol sweetie, I've never been loved so completely as you have and continue to love me from your depths. I see you are embarking on a new era of caring more deeply for yourself as I am. And that part of your way with me was out of fear of loss. And in the end you feel you have lost me, but to tell you the truth, you have the unfettered real me within anytime. And it's more beautiful now than it ever was in the body or the personality. Our love, our real love is pure and always present. Lean on me, my darling. I will hold you up—be by your side and within your heart.

More

My darling Carol,

You're so right. I was holding on to the unfulfilled dreams. As long as I had all the stuff, I would be able to dream of the day when I would be free. I couldn't guess it would turn out this way, and I'm sorry it bogged you down so much. I didn't want that for you. I just couldn't face the reality that we would never have a place of our own, never live out on our own, never give of myself to Mother Earth. Grandfather did that, and he was one with the earth and the sky and everything in the universe. My hero.

You, my darling, are my heroine today—you are reading me loud and clear. Thank you for giving me voice. It warms my heart to still be connected to you, my sweetie wife.

You're welcome, my tall, handsome, smart, sexy, cute, adorable husband. In all this we are one. Still now and forever.

November 9, 2010, Carol writes

In my relationships I related to the other person as myself. I was unable to see into Kenny for himself. I did not even think to ask him why he needed his compulsions. I just thought he was selfish and unwilling and procrastinating. This showed me the limitations in my thinking. Makes me afraid of myself in relationship with others. How shallow I have been. Not shallow really, just bound up in habitual responses. Faith will light the way.

—Teresa—

Hi, Carol,

You are totally amazing. The courage, patience, and unending love that you seem to have to share your journey with us, continues to move my heart. It's been quite a ride and still is... I am blessed every time I read one of your blogs.

God Bless you

—Cheryl Ann—

Carol, thank you for putting your experience into words. I remember and re-experience some of my process since my husband passed, also of cancer, eleven years ago. So familiar... it is a most rich time on so many levels. I honor your sharing so openly. With much gratitude and Light...

—Esther—

Oh Carol, this took me back to my own memories of Ken—he had many more interests than I knew about. How bravely you're walking through it all, Carol.

Chapter 39

Where Do I Go from Here? From Mourning to Conversations with Kenny

Carol, October 29, 2010

I was going to write about the huge impact having an attitude of gratitude plays in my life because in those months of caring for Kenny, there were so many miracles to be thankful for, and so many people who ministered to us on a daily basis. That would have been very uplifting and genuinely sweet and touching, after all, writing about being grateful to people for their generosity of Spirit and being grateful to God for the many moments of perfection we experienced, opens not only my heart, but most likely your heart as well. Only since my last entry, it's taken weeks of self-reflection, giving in to the never-ending tears, and beginning somatic therapy to even write the first sentence here. Having the notion of learning about perfection on my life path, I squander energy racing back and forth between feeling sorry for myself, grieving all by myself, putting on a face for my friends and coworkers so I won't appear self-indulgent. Feeling guilty that I haven't gotten past some fake and made up idea of a corner-turning stage of grief into a happier, more productive, more social, more likable, all healed up widow, ready to put Kenny in his rightful place in my memories and move on in my life to new beginnings. Widow! Always was a disturbing term, now it's downright mean.

I've intimated in previous posts that Kenny had a lot to hide. And he was a master at it. But what I didn't know is how much I was hiding. Throughout our marriage and probably throughout my entire life and all the other relationships I've had, I spent an inordinate amount of time and energy "fixing" my partners. This resulted in the ironic effect of keeping understanding and healing my own traumas at bay, avoiding any resolution for the last six decades. I thought of myself as the healthy one and I thought of the other as the helpless one, the sick one, the disturbed one, the one that needed "fixing." And if I only did thus and such, they would mend their ways and emerge one hundred percent recovered. Oh, and did I forget to say, in the emerging they would love me?

Where in the world did this come from? What made me the "fixer"? I can only speak to this lifetime, though I'm sure it stems from others. And I'm about to launch into psychobabble, so bear with me. When I was six months old, my father was called to World War II. So in November 1943, we packed all our gear, and Mommy and her "little monkey," as I was called, followed Daddy across country as far west as we could go before he was shipped off to the China/Burma/India theater. It was a brutal two years of ugly hand-to-hand combat, but he survived (only physically) and came home in 1945 a broken man. Friends and family whispered that Luddy—Lodovico Natale Colombi; "Luddy" (Christmas) Colombi—used to be so happy-go-lucky, and now, poor man, he sleeps a lot and his eyes look so sad, and he doesn't talk much anymore.

Somehow it was while Daddy was at war that I began to know myself as the "fixer." I was there to fix my mother's grief and fear of the ever-impending notice of injury or God forbid, death of her soldier-husband. I was glued to her side as if I hadn't been born yet. I absorbed her thoughts and feelings. I made her feel better just by giving her someone special to love. This would be a beautiful ministry for a little baby, but the bond became so impenetrable that when Daddy came home, there were no threads to unravel, no holes to peek into, not a smidgen of dust to indicate a draft where he might discover the path to relate to me.

Being the only child (a girl child) and wanting desperately to win my father's love, I remember following him around, asking to do things with him. I'd go up on the roof to hammer shingles down. I'd help him carry bricks when he built the outdoor barbecue, I'd ride with him in this '52 Ford pick-up to "colored town" to pay his helpers or pick them up on Monday morning after a weekend of bingeing. I'd try to be a boy to see if that would work. And I'd buy him presents I thought he would love for his birthday and Christmas, which by the way were the same day. Lodovico Natale Colombi. Luddy (Christmas) Colombi.

There it was, the beginning of a pattern of relating to men— who needed help. And it didn't stop there. My mother was sick most of my childhood with recurring bouts of Crohn's disease that required multiple surgeries almost like clockwork. If it was February—her birthday month—she was almost always in the hospital. Me, I had my share of childhood diseases, but nothing that didn't mend quickly and easily. There's so much history around so many childhood experiences, suffice it to say no wonder my darling Kenny was with me for only thirteen years and agreed in Spirit to leave me after the most traumatic year of our lives, but to leave me, never to be seen again on this earth. No calling to say I'm sorry, I'm coming home. No letters to say what he couldn't say in person, no repairing our marriage, no coming home from the war, just the end of all ends—death—the thing my mother feared the most. The thing I absorbed through my skin. In the end, in my pores, I knew they would all leave me.

See? I told you I feel self-indulgent, wallowing in my loss, stuck on repeat with no end in sight. And don't you wonder what somatic therapy will do for me? It's supposed to heal traumas, physical, emotional, mental, all of them. And I've had many more than the average first world citizen. So while some people get sick as a result of karmic patterns, others hurt themselves or allow others to hurt them. So my goal? To heal the hurts and change the karmic flow to create more balance—eh, maybe add to be happier, to experience more joy, and receive more love, and to absolutely know that God and I are one.

Meanwhile, I pour over the thousands of pictures my photographer-husband took over his lifetime, culling out the most beautiful and spectacular landscape photos and portraits of all his work in order to find a representative selection to include on the book website. Not only do I want to convey his magnificent transformation and transcendence through his own blog entries, but my own experiences of caring for him, grieving for him, growing my Self and learning to tune in to his messages from the Spirit world. I am convinced his ministry continues, and I want to know how and why and what he wants you, dear readers, to know about conscious death and conscious dying and the afterlife.

I am blessed to have this medium to share our precious story. God bless you and all your loved ones. I'd promise you that the next entry will be on gratitude, but we'll see. In the meantime, my dear friend who introduced me to Liz who introduced me to Ruthie, who is able to communicate with Kenny and all those who will teach me the same, encouraged me to include a picture of Kenny and me. Underneath, surrounding, and overriding all our challenges, is a deep and abiding love that no trauma could or would shake. It's there for eternity—a spiritual promise—our heritage as initiates and ministers of God. Look for it in these photos. And soon I'll be chatting away with Kenny myself.

Sending you all deepest love and gratitude for hanging in here with me, sending your love and Light, and witnessing the transformation of consciousness into the Heart of God.

Carol and Kenny August 1996 at the Jones
Family's Beloved Island House

—Esther—

I appreciate what you're revealing about yourself, Carol. Much I certainly never knew or even suspected. Makes me wonder what I may be hiding too.

November 3, 2010,
Message from Kenny, a day after
our wedding anniversary

Dear Kenny, are you with me today?

My darling Carol, I loved that we watched the wedding video last night. In my heart of hearts I meant every word of our vows. I trusted that you wouldn't leave me even though you were given cause in the made-up world we live in. But in the Spirit world we are one and there was a bond we both agreed to that was the most precious gift I have ever been given in your undying love and devotion. I always say and I always mean you are the love of my life, my sweetheart and my soul mate.

I love you, darling. Always remember we are betrothed in the high realms. Tears of joy stream from my eyes as I behold the beauty of your big heart. And thanks for the healing work last night. I needed that education. Keep tuning into my presence and we shall continue to create together.

I love the book. Keep going. God bless you, my one and only,

Kenny

Chapter 40

Through Kenny's Eyes

Carol, November 19, 2010

It's taken several weeks of viewing Kenny's photographs to find the right portrait of him to open the book. What was I looking for among the many photos of him throughout the years? As I said in the introduction, I was told that in Spirit he is his youthful, strong, healthy self and to imagine him that way when I want to touch into his soul. And I would add, as I often remarked to him, he was my "tall, smart, witty, sexy," and yes, "strong and healthy hero." This portrait was taken in 1979 and conveys not only those attributes but also his friendly, helpful, always smiling, light-hearted nature. Oh yes, he had his dark moments, but that's not who he really is. Who he really is mirrors the attributes of the soul and uplifts those around him.

Sink into that forever smile!

See what I mean? I want you to see it now in this chapter where I begin to tell you how I'm learning to refine my ranging into the spiritual realms in order to meet Kenny where he is. The dual outcome will be not only to meet him where he is, but to be more closely in touch with my own soul. To uncover the joy and all the good things of the soul. To live them consciously. To be able to share what I'm doing so anyone else can do the same thing.

Before I close this chapter, I want you to know that I just found an unpublished piece that Kenny wrote on February 10, 2010, just about six weeks before he took his final breath. Here it is, a remarkable observation of where he saw himself physically and how he experienced himself spiritually. My hero indeed.

Kenny said:

I look at my future now and I see that my physical body is very close to dropping into the Well of the Souls. There are so many signs of deterioration, degeneration, and decay in my body that it's a wonder I'm still walking around. I'm pretty sure that my oncologist has seen melanoma take down so many people that he has formed a picture of what it looks like at each step along the way, and has a head movie of the *Melanoma Melodrama from Start to Finish*. The finish looks the same whether patients opt for chemotherapy or not. The only differences are

1. How long it takes to die (and that is measured in one, two, three months, etc.)
2. How ugly the dead patient is. More ugly with chemo.
3. The quality of life the patient enjoyed or endured. Chemo patients sometimes unwittingly, and perhaps sometimes, in an effort to avoid pain or increase security, have chosen a path of suffering that actually makes life less attractive than the release from the concentrated body pain currently going on.

As one who never opted for any form of chemo, I can say that my quality of life has steeply increased as my disease has steadily progressed. I feel as though I am among the "living free." I have so little standing between me and my awareness of God that practically all I see is beauty. I take meds to control the pain, and I handle the basic body functions to keep it going, and my consciousness dances free in the Light of God.

Kenny's story is extraordinary. As John Morton coined, his "ministry is on fire."

—Esther—

What Kenny says about being among the living free, and so aware of God that practically all he sees is beauty— that's enlightenment, isn't it? I wonder if he had a sense of what an inspiring writer he could be... Wish we had much more of what was going on in his head, his consciousness, in that last year.

Light to your whole project, Carol!

—Jeanne—

Love the photo and the post. This made me weep as usual. Painful on some levels, glorious on others. Such important areas to explore, but hard to look at too. Sending you lots of love and Light.

My mom just lost her beloved husband of more than thirty-seven years to cancer in November. They are and were amazing examples of living love, but sadly they do not believe in an afterlife (though I think in their hearts they hope it is true). I think that makes things harder when the focus is on the body and death as a finality.

So many people miss the opportunities that you and Kenny write/wrote about. So hard in this world to stay conscious with dying, grief, mourning and spiritual blessings in the process. Not sure I can do it... takes such courage. I find it hard to accept that everyone I love will die on me or I will die on them, so I mostly try not to think about that. Perhaps grief is just a deep longing for our own soul, Light, love, God, and oneness.

—Carol replied—

Thank you so much for your support. This blog is launching into some kind of book in which Kenny teaches about conscious dying, I share my process of grieving and how it moves into celebrating the precious relationship we still have, unencumbered by the body, mind, and emotions. It emerges as pure, unconditional loving, joy, upliftment and oneness. I have such depth of experience to draw on, it's inevitable that this last year will springboard me into realizing finally what J-R has been teaching us for so long—my desire to consciously reach up into the high soul realms is becoming as strong as wanting my next breath. My impetus—meeting Kenny on the level he is experiencing now, which according to messages so far is bliss, is unconditional loving, is service, is profound, is rest in the arms of the Lord, is no-words-can-describe home.

My loving and gratitude reaches out to you and blesses you.

Chapter 41

Maybe I Should Just Kill Myself

Carol, November 22, 2010

A couple of months before the cancer diagnosis, we were arguing about what I called unnecessary spending. Me and my "volunteer" salary and Kenny on unemployment. When I couldn't get through, when I felt unheard, when I resorted to mad, mean, sarcastic retort, I yelled almost red-faced, "Get a job!" To that he said, "Maybe I should just kill myself."

I was in shock… utter disbelief, insurmountable shame, that my words could evoke such a powerful response. I still had no clue how much turmoil was boiling under that calm, deliberate, and plodding exterior. But immediately I too felt the impact I meant for him and cried out, "Oh no, honey, I didn't mean for you to go there." I'm so sorry, my darling, my tall, strong, handsome, cute, smart, sexy adorable husband. But still, even though I pulled back my rage, my temper, my "fresh" and stabbing comment for which in my childhood I would have been smacked in the mouth and punished, I still didn't get how powerful his cry for help was. How could I have known only two months later he would be sentenced to death by metastasized melanoma cancer? Little was I aware of how his body had already been ravaged by the disease without us even having one clue. No pain, no bulging tumors, no erupting moles, and yet there it was, silently killing my husband, the negative power having its way with his precious body, imprisoning his mind and emotions. Even this was hiding, and lurking, and eating him alive.

This moment of taking back my rage opened a place in me that saw, for the first time in a way that I could put words on it, how entwined I was in his family karma. I responded to him a lot like he told me they responded to his perceived weaknesses. Of course, he fit perfectly into mine as well. What that looked like is yet to be discovered. The point here is that in my realization, a thin trail opened before me and as I stepped out of the forest into the clearing, there I found my compassionate heart, and I began to see what he was reacting to in me—the judgmental, scolding, nothing's-good-enough wife-mother-father-family all rolled into one.

So instead of blaming him for not having a job, for spending money frivolously, for amassing huge quantities of stuff, I began to have compassion for his story. So while all these years my ranting and raving had no appreciable effect, this one single nanosecond of compassion opened up a whole new world of discovery. My God, it does work to take baby steps. And another of the precious teachings of the Spiritual Heart reveals itself to me.

What did I discover? By now it was only a month or so before the diagnosis, and life as we knew it was about to change unmistakably, irrevocably, and permanently. What's the lesson here? If you keep on doing the thing that is not working, you'll get what's not working. If you change just an iota, a hair's breath, a blink of an eye, new worlds of opportunity become available. If you remind yourself that unconditional loving is the foundation for a deep and abiding relationship, and by the way is always there underneath all the fodder of the world, it's just a matter of shoveling that fodder into a pile where God can transform it into gold. You'd spend much less time, if any fooling around with reactions to negativity that cause it to fester instead of dissolve, and more time in the Heart of God expressing the "good things of the soul"—unconditional loving, compassion, understanding, acceptance, and a list a mile long of positive responses to life's beauty and life's challenges.

I leave you with a heart full of gratitude for all the gifts I am heir to in this unprecedented era of awakening in my life. The greatest portion of the gratitude goes to my sweet and adorable husband who in a pure, selfless act of generosity, gave his life in service to my awakening. I know that's not all that happened and he didn't die just for me, and then again, maybe he did. After all, we were told that we assisted each other to pass into the realms of Spirit many lifetimes before. No wonder this was *the* most profound experience of my life—a culmination of eons of passing with his dear and precious soul, and certainly, as John-Roger has prepared us for our final and most important transition of our lives, it was the most profound and beautiful experience of this lifetime for Kenny. I am left in awe and give thanks for it all.

—Esther—

What truth in the observation that if I change just one iota, if I can create inside myself one tiny millimeter of compassion space, the whole course of the interaction/relationship/situation can change. But to find that crack inside, there's the challenge. Guess that's where stepping back and remembering, "I love you. God bless you. Peace be still." might help. Beautiful post.

—Millicent—

In acknowledgment of your soul sharing, awakening to divine loving, and breathtaking awareness of the real self I salute you, love you, and stand with you in all of God's glory. beloved one. Yours all ways.

Chapter 42

Kenny Asked Me to Write Something Wonderful about Him

Carol, December 24, 2010

I said I would write this post about my husband's wonderful qualities, since in previous posts, I revealed the challenges we had as a couple working our relationship to the best of our abilities. That's always so hard to remember when we're in the thick of it. Not only us, but the generations before us and the ones to come—we're all always doing the best we can, such as it is. And that deserves to be loved and to be shown compassion and understanding and acceptance. What stands in the way of those qualities of the soul? Judgment, self-judgment, judging others without really knowing what's in their hearts and how challenging it may be for them to access their heart of hearts. So here I am, reinforcing for my own edification, my husband's wonderful and positive qualities.

Kenny would say, "Come out here and look at the moon, Carol. It's almost full." In other words "I can't wait for it to be full. Then I can't wait for it to be a sliver again. Then full again. I never tire of being awestruck in the presence of the moon, hanging bright over a cloudless sky. The wilderness pulls me all the time to its peace and serenity. I'm at home there. I feel the earth and the creatures, and I innately understand them and me as one. I love my campsite in the mountains. I go there whenever

I can. I challenge myself to not just survive in the pristine and rugged terrain, but to thrive in it. It's cold most nights, and I cover myself with as little as I can while my simple campfire warms me just enough. I love the pines and the boulders, and the air as I breathe in God's gift."

And the clouds in the sky. What a magnificent show God and Mother Earth put on for us. Billowing, puffy white clouds, streaming cottony strings of clouds, thunder clouds—I love the rain, he would say. And the wind. Stir up the air and Kenny was happy. Have I mentioned yet that he survived Hurricane Iniki on Kauai in 1992? Did I tell you the one about the car trip where he pulled us out of a giant squeeze between two semis in our little Honda CRV? Unscathed! Except for the adrenalin coursing through our veins and seizing our nervous systems.

He loved horse races and stories about racing. I'd look over at him while we were watching and tears would be streaming down his face. What was that? I would ask. He'd have that sheepish grin filled with innocence and wonder. "I love the race, the magnificence of the horse. I feel God's presence in the race, in being the best one can be, in outrunning my own personal best." He was an athlete in his youth, sprinting, hurdling, and swimming, footballing, and all the rest. In funny moments he would make us laugh by isolating just about any muscle in his body including wiggling one ear at a time. That's how trained his body was.

Kenny loved to learn. What a voracious appetite for information, and putting that stuff to good use. He devoured books on just about anything that interested him. And he could recite any part of it to the amazement of those who cared to listen. See chapter 38, the Yard Sale chapter, and you'll read all about what he loved.

Handsome's not good enough. The electric magnetism of his bright blue eyes, the soulful gaze. The forever turned-up smile. He was always welcoming and warm. And helpful to anyone that asked. He had a natural flirtatious look, not pretentious and not fake. All of that made me fall in love with him despite his wiggling ears!

What about tenderness? Whenever we watched a tender scene in a movie or on TV, or listened to a meaningful song, he would make a point to hug me or hold my hand or otherwise show me he was touched and wanted to share his heart with me. Of course I melted—every time.

Well 'nough said tonight on this subject, although it doesn't take much to get me to talk about him, to think about him, and to try to accept that he is gone from this physical world. It's the intimacy of a companion that I miss. Coming home to him or welcoming him home. Saying I love you and snuggling to share a good night's sleep. Waking and then meditating together. The closeness of being with each other day by day, and planning for the future, and telling each other about our dreams, the ones we have at night and the ones we have when we're awake.

Mostly there was an unspoken bond that held us to each other even in the tough times when others would have let go. The commitment of one soul to the other soul, the marriage vows that specifically promised we'd go into the Heart of God together. Little did I know he would go so soon, but even now I understand that he will be assisting me to reach up into the high realms where his radiant form resides to find my own soul and experience it fully while I'm still here traversing this life on Earth. Love is eternal. Love is unconditional. Love is all there is.

Chapter 43

Remembrance Day for Kenny

Carol, April 2011

My dear friends and family,

March 30 marked one year since my sweet, funny, handsome, talented, mischievous, and darling husband left his body to go home to God. I knew I wanted to have some kind of acknowledgment of that day, though since we had already had three memorials in 2010, it didn't seem appropriate to have yet another memorial. As I projected in my mind what would sooth my healing heart, I realized I wanted an intimate gathering of those who seemed to make a big difference in our experience near the end of his life. I'm sure there were many others whose silent prayers and distant caring impacted us deeply, so choosing whom to invite was a challenge. But the place was very clear to me. It would be Gail's house, the site of many patio dinners and movies and Christmas Eves, and Thanksgiving dinners. The fare would be Kenny's favorites, and the emphasis would be on acknowledging the loving and caring poured out to us at a time when every minute and every breath counted. I called it Remembrance Day.

Here's what I wrote to Kenny's sisters, who all live on the East Coast and whom I wanted to include as much as I could.

Remembrance Day was a very dear and sweet gathering of people who assisted Kenny and me on an ongoing basis, and friends who loved him very much. We had it at Gail's house. I purposely chose Gail's because she has a very sweet little place on the west side. And Gail, Yvonne, Kenny, and I were pals and did things together including that trip to Northern California in winter of 2008. And many of the furnishings in her house Kenny helped her assemble. I brought with me some of his favorite music and the two pictures of him in his youth that I love—the close-up on the beach at twenty-three, and the one in the engineer's cap in his early thirties. Plus I brought an enlargement of the one of all of you and Kenny dressed in blue in front of the Island House. I also brought the album you all put together, which everyone loved looking through. The living room was crammed full with only seventeen people—just as I imagined it would be—cozy, close, chairs all lined up like a couch.

Here's how the day went:

I opened with a prayer and asked for Kenny's soul to be present.

I acknowledged each person present for their personal giving—said something personal to each one. Many brought tears and choked words, but I felt it important to acknowledge each one.

I read Kenny's ministerial ordination blessing. In MSIA ministers have special callings that amplify their strengths and gifts. In Kenny's case, the focus is on his "storehouse of treasures," empathy, compassion, kindness and sensitivity—not in grand gestures, but in simple ways that show people he cares. And it encourages him to share his healing touch. I especially wanted everyone there to hear it because from my experience, he exemplified this blessing in his last few months more evidently than ever before.

You asked me to tell everyone that his family loved him very much and still does. I did that and showed everyone the family photo. There were audible sighs of empathy and appreciation in the group. Most of them had met you when you came to visit in

January 2010. And they remembered the Jones sense of humor. Remember Kenny in those New Jersey crab shorts!

John Morton, our spiritual director, came to visit Kenny just a week or so before he passed and was so uplifted by his exuberance, he told Kenny his ministry was on fire! Kenny's response was, "If people could discover what I'm experiencing, they'd drop what they are doing and do what I'm doing!" This visit was recorded, and at this point in the gathering, I played the recording of what Kenny said. Hearing his voice, especially with such a poignant message, brought tears to people's eyes. They realized how much they missed him. Everyone realized he was showing us how to leave this world gracefully, in love and excitement and gratitude.

Kenny's favorite recording artist and song writer is Mark Knopfler. At this point I played Knopfler's "Remembrance Day," which is how I came to name the gathering. Knopfler is British, and in England, Remembrance Day is like our Memorial Day, commemorating our fallen soldiers. The song is on the album *Get Lucky*, Knopfler's latest at the time, with many poignant songs that Kenny loved and I had grown to love. On YouTube there is clip of Knopfler singing this song (http://www.youtube.com/watch?v=CBPSr4TsQkI).

Then lots of people shared their fond memories of Kenny. It was very sweet and actually fun to hear it all. It reminded me of lolling in the pool at your house in Bayhead, as we all told stories the night after Kenny's orchestration of his ashes day. (This is cited in chapter 35, The Funeral Train Began in Springfield.)

I ended the formal part of the gathering with Kenny's poem about the Prana gardens. Writing this poem was one of his moments of empathy and sensitivity. And reading it was even more so. He paused in just the right places, emphasizing the delightful scene he was weaving. I'm adding it here:

Morning Observations in Peace
Awareness Labyrinth and Gardens
July 21, 2004
by Ken Jones

Photo by Ken Jones

Cool morning air,
thick with blossom smell,
caresses me inside and out.
Inside the delicate delightful green garden
sweet tendrils of tenderness
tell me I am loved.
Birds flitting, humming, and peering
sing and call their kin:

"Here I am, here I am here I am.
"Come nest with me, come nest with me.
"Let's eat, let's eat, let's eat.
"Boy, I'm glad...
glad glad glad glad glad!"
The goldfish and koi and their playmates
glide in schools of silence
and rejoice...
in the suspended...
Current...
of... the... pond...
Every moment the arcing sunlight brings fresh beauty,
whether illuminating lush leaves,
or reflecting ripples
that tickle tall translucent trunks.
Outside the green garden bubble,
the world rushes on,
Leaving us alone in soft splendid grace.
Once again I know gratitude.

Then we had homemade pound cake with Häagen-Dazs vanilla ice cream. Two of Kenny's favorites.

It was very warming and satisfying to create this gathering. For me it felt like Kenny was right there with us saying something like, "I had no idea so many people cared about me." Well I know we all did and we all do still.

I hope you enjoyed this homage. Every holiday, birthday, and anniversary will have passed this coming Wednesday, March 30. I don't know what the next year will hold, but I do know I'm missing Kenny and you all as well.

December 12, 2010

Happy Birthday, Kenny,

I love you so much and I'm seeing you young and healthy and full of life and Joy. How are you seeing yourself today, my love?

Hi, honey—I love you, and thanks for finding the feather—I put it there so you'd see it today. What a joy to watch you find it. Your tears still are so endearing to me. I'm fine, resting from some intense work here on this side of things. They are teaching me many things—not the least of which is to fly through the realms. Like the dreams I used to have. Then I can be by your side in an instant. I love being by your side. When you go to sleep at night I lie next to you and watch you breathe. You are so peaceful and lovely.

I'm having a great birthday. I visited my siblings today and saw them remembering me. It was very dear. Send everyone the Light. They are all doing their best at any time. And I know they love me in their own way and it's all perfect. No worries, no concerns. Gotta go now, but I love that you are celebrating me. Keep a positive focus and soon we'll be flying together.

Sometimes you don't even have to ask Spirit for anything. It answers your unspoken prayer instantly. All you have to do is think something and Spirit's response comes rushing in like a wild hurricane. You say, "My God, everything is breaking loose around me. My life is opening up. All the things that I could ever dream of are happening. It's wonderful!"

Yes it is. That's the Inner Master, the Traveler, saying to you, "We're here, we're present, what can we do for you?" Be smart and ask for love to fill your life and to know the presence of God. Those are the only things that have value.

—John-Roger

Chapter 44

My Life Partner Is Gone— My Awakening Begins

May 30, 2011

My life partner is gone. At our wedding, we promised each other we would go into the heart of God together. We said:

I promise to love you unconditionally
no matter what lessons and gifts God lays down before us
to support you in times of sorrow and of joy
to minister to you when you are in need
to honor the true, the beautiful, and the Divine within you
to share my life openly and freely with you
to be your one and only lover and your best friend
to go together into the heart of God
with the loving and guidance of Jesus
Christ and the Mystical Traveler
and to remain your loyal and faithful
companion through it all.
Spirit give me the strength to live my life whole
with you [Spirit] leading the way, and
my beloved Kenny by my side.
"Baruch Bashan," the blessings already are.

Good grief, who channeled these promises? What did we expect of each other? Who could live up to those vows? There's no doubt we worked at it. We apologized almost daily for many transgressions. We participated in workshops, counseling, classes, and we cleared ourselves energetically as best we could. We did almost everything together, hand in hand, soul and soul.

Yet there was a huge gap in our daily experience of loving each other and the knowing in our hearts that our love was slated and we were fulfilling our destiny together. What was that gap about? It was the result of the traumas we each experienced in our lives before we met. And the behaviors we unconsciously perpetuated in service to self-preservation.

What were my traumas? What could cloud the deepest love I have ever experienced in this lifetime? What could set the wedges gashing at our hearts? Whatever they were from infancy to adulthood, they added up to a frozen nervous system, habitually set on fight or flight or alternatively frozen like a deer staring into oncoming headlights.

What were his? I couldn't guess the earlier ones. I did hear about the near-death experience of Hurricane Iniki though, and I did hear about the near helicopter crash. Oh, and I did hear a bit about the physical, emotional, and mental challenges as a child.

At once we came to each other in innocence, and we came to each other tainted by our life experiences. How could that be? It's called unconscious. It's running on rote, ignoring the signs of destruction, falling head over heels in love no matter how many red flags were hoisted. In either direction, mind you—pointed at him, pointed at me. We were a perfect match of innocents seeking to be rescued. In his dream, I was to usher him into the Soul Realm, and in my dream, he was to enfold me in his unconditional love forever, taking the place of the father who went off to war and came back damaged by the ravages of hand-to-hand combat, emotionally scarred, his own brand of frozen-in-time.

All the plans, the dreams, the patience, and forgiveness. All the vacations and road trips, the house hunting and furniture buying.

The trips back to the beloved Island House, site of a lifetime of yearly family reunions. Too few years together. Too young to die. And most of all, too young to leave me alone—yet again.

Kenny's death catapulted me into an entirely new era of my life. I miss him terribly and wish all the learning I've done since he passed didn't require him to have passed. But while we were both in the physical body, we were frozen in our responses to each other's weaknesses. Locked into a set reaction that neither assisted nor moved us. So to say we were stuck in our own private miasma is just about accurate.

The remedy: I'd been through Reichian therapy, bioenergetics, psychodrama, MSIA spiritual counseling. I'd studied in MSIA for years, became an initiate and minister, graduated from Temple University, University of Santa Monica, and Peace Theological Seminary with master's degrees, and after all that psychological work and soul searching, still my body held on to measured responses, to unpredictable reactions of rage and defense, to lashing out and withholding love and truth, and an aloofness that belied the longing for closeness and intimacy. But this time, I was all too aware of what seemed like lifetimes of a kind of pain that surely derived from welled up sadness and anger, welled up loss and betrayal. Welled up abandonment. If only one of these modalities worked. Wouldn't that be a miracle.

So in my quest for healing, peace, deeper understanding, love, and compassion for myself, after Ken's passing, I found somatic therapy, which gave me space and time to grieve in a way that allowed me to understand and have deeper compassion for my life patterns.

In the meantime, those vows we took were to manifest themselves fully and completely during the last nine months of Kenny's life, so much so that we became as one being, headed straight for God's heart on a supersonic shuttle. I've said it so many times before in many different ways, inventing different word phrases and conjuring different metaphors in an effort to describe the indescribable. The love, the spiritual energy, were palpable. The constant companionship played like the colors in a Monet landscape, the taking care of each other looked like a storybook fairy tale of true love. And it was. The going into the heart of God part was evident each day as Kenny neared his passing. He got closer to God with measured breaths now, and took me with him on the most magnificent journey any of us could ever imagine, that all of us will someday experience ourselves. I only hope I have the consciousness, the sense of adventure, and the willingness to let go and let God that Kenny demonstrated.

Today he's among the souls watching over us from other worlds. He makes his presence known through his sweetness, his sense of humor, his love of nature. All his sisters, many of our friends, and I sense his essence is often near.

―――

—Sandra—

> Once again I find myself humbled and honored to be witness to your journey. You mentioned in your post that Kenny has showed us how to leave this world "in love and excitement and gratitude." I want to acknowledge that you continue to show us how to say good-bye—with that same grace.
>
> My love to you and Kenny

―――

Near our wedding anniversary, I gathered housemates to honor Kenny's memory and our marriage. Hey, Kenny, did you like everyone seeing our wedding video tonight and eating lemon poppy-seed pound cake?

> My sweetie wife, I loved our ceremony. I loved our vows. You certainly kept them better than I did. Carol, I had serious problems that I never wanted you to see. I was

wrong to hide so much but driven by entities that pushed me over the edge every day. They compelled me to hide it all so we could continue to be controlled by the dark forces. But there's no doubt I loved you then and even more now. And there's no doubt you held us together just like our vows said. And I didn't leave either—the bond was too strong. Now I can help you find someone who'll have capacities I didn't have. It will be a different kind of love but very fulfilling in its own way. The karma will be different—more around choice instead of compulsion. My heart was always open to you, sweet wife. My tears showed you the depth of my love. I meant all those times straight from my heart to yours. God bless you, Carol. You are in my heart of hearts, my one and only lover, my best friend.

Come to me often, and I will assemble the angels whenever you ask.

Wedding Day November 2, 1996

—From Brooke Thompson after Michael died—

Thank you, Carol. Michael wrote so many beautiful prayers, and I have found comfort in many of them, particularly the ones he wrote just before he died. When you read those, it is hard to believe he had no idea he would be passing so soon. I truly appreciate your loving and kind thoughts and Light and prayers. We both lost our true loves, and it is a sisterhood I would rather not be a member of to be honest, but if I am to be a member, I am glad to have friends and sisters like you to help me get through.

Loving you so much
Brooke

Chapter 45

Have I Ever Said I'm Sorry to Myself?

Carol, August 31, 2011

I haven't made an entry in several months. I've been deeply experiencing the changes in my consciousness due to a strengthened nervous system. Have watched myself respond differently to stress, differently to the unexpected, differently to what before might have caused me to react negatively. Yet I haven't known what to write. Remember, I am still reeling from the effects of my Kenny's illness and death. A whole new era of my life has opened up, for which he prepared me, outfitted me to the hilt by allowing me to learn unconditional love and unconditional service, selfless service for the last nine months of his life. This constant positive input culminating with his conscious death and glorious ascension into the heart of God was like shooting me out of a cannon—a wildly targeted blast to my consciousness.

While I miss him still, even after all these months, I can only move forward, processing the new awarenesses, the new behaviors, the new thoughts and emotions, the greater capacity to love and forgive. In my marriage, I didn't have the courage to face my own demons, so I spent inordinate energy, time, frustration, and upset trying to fix Kenny's demons. They at least had names. Mine were so hidden I couldn't name them, let alone define them and work with them. Now don't you find that pretty stupid? Haven't you heard it said so many times over your lifetime that you cannot change anyone else? Well I have, too. Honestly! Many times! But being locked into a deeply embedded channel of reactivity, scarred by multiple traumas to my nerve pathways throughout at least this lifetime provided the blinders that matched Kenny's blinders perfectly. Isn't karma wonderful! Well okay, hindsight is 20-20, right? I'm not saying all this to berate myself, more that I am in awe of how karma works. How locked in we can get when we don't want to see. We don't want to move. We don't want to risk change or even just look at the truth.

My somatic therapist asked me during one of my sessions if I had compassion for myself. I had to think, and then I said I had spent a lot of time regretting my actions or non-actions, or wishing I had more consciousness to do things differently. That compassion came painstakingly and only rarely. In my doctor of spiritual science class, my classmate Rama asked me if I've ever told myself I'm sorry for past actions and judgments. I had to say no, I hadn't.

I had been taught about self-forgiveness in my spiritual practices—to forgive myself for judging myself, not for past actions, since what good would it do to judge an action that had already taken place, but for the judgment I placed on myself, which still sits in here buffering me against my will. But I never thought to tell myself I'm sorry for these actions. So if I could encourage you to do one thing, it would be to forgive yourself for judging yourself. It's about caring enough for myself to apologize for the less than highest good actions that I either planned myself or promoted by virtue of abdication of my responsibility to myself. And the ones I incurred because of ignorance or not taking myself and my conditions seriously enough or out of plain unawareness, if that's a word—it's an important one in my book of metaphors.

So via somatic therapy tools, I'm broadcasting this across all systems on all levels of consciousness including my physical body, and I'm telling every cell of my being all about the love and compassion I am now experiencing for myself and for others. The reptilian mind is being soothed. It can distinguish much more clearly between actual danger and perceived danger and it acts more according to the current situation instead of being locked into fight or flight.

My somatic practices make space in my consciousness every day for deep breaths, for anchoring in the new behaviors, for being okay with any feelings or thoughts that may be disturbing, all because I have the tools now to move me from disturbance to okay-ness. And at times I can even move from okay-ness to joy. They call it being resilient. Isn't that a wonderful term? Being able to bounce back, even being able to see the good in the disturbance (learn the lesson). And isn't that what life is all about anyway? From the higher perspective, with a physical body, mind, and emotions in tow, the soul incarnates to learn and to usher itself back into the heart of God. If one can do that while still on the planet, it's a lesson in learning how to die from this world every day through spiritual exercises, and finally in the end through leaving the body behind for the last time.

Down here on earth, I pray every day for resilience, compassion, heartfelt expression, and just plain loving myself and everyone and everything else. Big order, I know. One day at a time, one acknowledgement at a time. One apology at a time.

———

To someone who asked if it is okay to take one's own life, Carol said

I have been taught through my spiritual teachings that taking one's life is not a great idea. Why? Because the soul never dies, and if you drop this body before God has given you all the lessons and blessings planned for this life, then the soul has to pick up another body to continue the lesson. The lesson has to be learned before the soul is free of this world. So killing oneself doesn't solve anything. It only prolongs the lesson. Plus there's the trauma the new body has to deal with of having a previous life cut short.

—A reader—

Hi, thanks for sharing. I have been going through similar transformations as well. Like purpose, and all this stuff too much to mention. Dying in a metaphorical sense and rebirthing myself. Changes, acceptance. That there's something beyond this, that I am more, and yet how have I been an impediment at times to my own growth? It's true, I learn through crisis. I learn through having everything stripped away, all distractions so I can get to my highest good. And hopefully as I become more aware, I can stay there. I can be this person I'm meant to be without fear or feelings of ridicule.

—————

Many people whom I don't know have read the blog and some have commented. The teachings of the Spiritual Heart are reaching out through the blog and through this book to touch the lives of countless souls.

Chapter 46

Assuming the Contract Was Sealed in a Spiritual Promise

Carol, September 1, 2011

Assume Kenny and I agreed to work out our life lessons as husband and wife before we incarnated this lifetime—and I do. Assume his two previous marriages and my two previous marriages fulfilled the exact parts of these life lessons in the perfect ways they were supposed to—and I do. Assume we promised each other we would "go into the heart of God together," and we did. Promise that is. Go into the Heart of God together? That's what this writing is all about.

I've talked about the deepest love either of has ever known from a mate—the underlying glue that held us together on the highest levels. I've also talked about the miasma we were enmeshed in, the karmic flow, or in more descriptive terms, the energetic tableau. But I'm getting a deeper glimpse these last few days. Knowing we always do the best we can with who we are and what resources we have at the time, this is not about looking back with blame or regret. This is about looking into the consciousness for a deeper cut—a view from the unconditional love of the soul—a place of forgiveness and compassion.

With that said, I invite you to embrace the rest of this chapter from the same place.

Early in the marriage there were signs of "sandpapering," a kind term for conflict. Differences in how we functioned in the world as individuals. Some minor differences we were able to work with, but the essential, deep-seated, maybe even ancient patterns that one would consider weaknesses or character defects or more accurately blocks to spiritual awareness, were set in reactivity to each other. It was a perfect match. He was allowed to continue his unconscious avoidance of relating to me as his partner in such a way that allowed my unconscious avoidance to blind me to that which would unveil my next steps in my own spiritual growth. Oh we worked on "issues," we came to some agreements, we at least rose above the "you must-squeeze-the-toothpaste-tube-the-way-I-want-you-to" kinds of sandpapering.

But for those many years, fifteen to be exact, in secret he went his way and I avoided mine. I was so busy "handling" his much more obvious challenges, I couldn't see mine. Oh, I'd have glimpses (which probably scared the pants off me), and then I'd brush them aside. Sometimes I'd be completely resigned that our life together on these levels would never change, and I'd better just be happy with what we did have, not realizing, not having a clue, that if I would just change one thing about *me*, that would affect *us* dramatically.

So fear ran my relationship with Kenny—if I came to my senses, I would have to leave. Or surely he would leave me. Rather than risk that kind of change, I remained mired in my own participation in the miasma we had slipped into so silently.

Remember all this is seated in the traumatized nervous system. There was no escape. Patterns were set in frozen nerve pathways. Reactions were predictable and limited to those resulting in fighting or fleeing. As a result we ignored many opportunities in those glimpses to precipitate change. Because the gentler approach was not recognized or heeded many times over, God now set about preparing us for *the* most impactful experience of our lives. And this, from my view, was the purpose for the diagnosis of incurable, highly advanced, inoperable metastasized, malignant melanoma cancer—a three-to-six-month death sentence. If we, as a committed unit, didn't get it now, there would not be another chance.

In a flash, we were hurtled into action. Apologies for past indiscretions and hurts flew back and forth. We came into the oneness of Spirit, of seeing the path we were to take clearly and unmistakably. You could say the fear of death awakened us into positive action, leaving behind everything no longer in alignment with the goal—Kenny getting well again and loving ourselves and each other so completely that nothing else mattered. It was a beautiful experience of clarity of purpose.

I've written about this so many times. What strikes me now is that God so loved us, his children, that he made us in Jesus's likeness, that he would even snuff out the physical life of one of us in order to have us learn what we agreed to embrace before incarnating into these bodies. And here I sit, in complete and utter awe that this consciousness, this nervous system, held the old pattern of gripping so tightly that my darling husband would have to die, not just take a break, or leave my side, but forever die to this world for the last time in order for us both to take our next steps in realizing who we are. He would take those steps in the next world. I am left to take them here.

And I'm guessing he would say the same thing. "My consciousness, my nervous system, held on so dearly to my patterns, I would have to leave this world to meld with the Divine." And the process of leaving, from my vantage point, was what set him apart from all past actions, all patterns, all miasmas. In a blaze of glory, he left this world knowing who he was, who God is, and where he was going. We could not, in our wildest dreams, ask for a more graceful and tender goodbye.

Tears well up as I now look upon this story, this era of my life, with the compassion and loving that bring forth understanding and peace. The Spiritual Promise was fulfilled, and in our heart of hearts, we knew it would be. I stood by him as he ascended into the Heart of God, and I know he will be one of those ushering me on the same path when it's my time to go. It is with profound gratitude to my Kenny for sacrificing his life so that I may grow closer to God and closer to knowing I am one with God, closer to realizing my self that I write this and share it with you.

God bless us all.

—Gail—

Ms. Jones,

In the world of words, yours have become as high and extraordinarily perfect to the essence of who we are and aspire to recognize, as Martin Buber (a personal favorite), the astounding female mystics of spiritual catholic cloisters (like St. Catherine of Siena), and John-Roger. I love you for giving and sharing this with us all, my dear friend. And that is allowing for all the love I have for you as simply and wonderfully, my friend.

—A friend—

What a beautiful, clear perspective you have brought to the complexity of your relationship as the expression of a sacred contract. Your awakening into even greater wisdom is inspiring. Thank you for sharing at such a deep level.

If we, indeed, pay attention, even for one day out of our lifetimes, and we are, indeed, thoughtful and intuitive, and we are watching very carefully where we're putting our mind and our emotions and our body, we might not get much done that day in the physical, emotional, mental world, but we would deliver ourselves from eons of karma.

—John-Roger, *The Tao of Spirit*

Chapter 47

His Embrace—I'm in the Right Place at the Right Time, Doing the Right Thing

Carol, January 11, 2012

John Morton, spiritual director of MSIA and holder of the keys to the Mystical Traveler Consciousness, recently wrote the following and sent it to his "all" list.

A very dear friend brought their deepest grieving to me this first day of the Christ Mass. Here is what I found to say to them.

Merry Christ Mass

Let's look at the Good News.

Consider that at some point in your existence not so long ago that you invited the Beloved Christ/Traveler to dwell with you and also that you requested to be of service, to serve all, even unconditionally in your loving, caring and gifts of Spirit. Consider that now you are serving at the fount of grieving, surely your own from wherever it has become created and stored, and then in the Way that is the Light and the Truth, you are clearing and bringing the last of any grieving in the world to His Embrace. Be Glad. Be Joyous. Find the Celebration of Peace to All.

In previous chapters, I wrote about the depth of grief I experienced as Kenny neared his death. It began the very day we were told of his diagnosis and escalated every day until I could hardly bear it. I found myself saying (to myself only), "This pain I'm feeling is bigger than what's going on." As profound and shocking as it was to witness the daily loss of a piece of my husband's body, what was welling up inside me was bigger than I could fathom. And I also mentioned earlier that in a spiritual reading, Michael Hayes told us we had supported each other through the dying process in thirty-five previous lifetimes. That seemed to give me some understanding as to why my grief was so big.

Today in a spiritual retreat of MSIA staff, as John Morton was sharing with one of the staff here at MSIA headquarters, I was able to reach into the higher realms just a twinkle to glimpse one of the universal truths there. Mind you, it was just a blink, but it was like a Narnia tale. The secret door was opened into a whole new world of truth and grace. Here's what I figured out (or saw or heard—remember, my clairvoyant gift is in the mental realm, so it's hard for me to distinguish what's one of my thoughts and what's a truth)—but here goes!

If I can, as John Morton says, bring the last of any grieving in the world to His Embrace, I can also bring the last of any karmic action or habit or addiction or pattern, situation or circumstance to His Embrace from all the eons of my existences. And with the Traveler's help, I can stack those past experiences such that clearing one clears them all. And I don't even have to be conscious doing this. I just need to have the intention that it's possible. But as initiates of the Mystical Traveler I'm not even sure I need that. I just *am*!

And finally I understood from my own personal revelation that grace is present. That J-R's message of heaven here on earth while we are alive in our bodies is indeed possible. That through all the trials and tribulations of our karma, if we maintain the thread of happiness underneath it all, we emerge happy for it all, living in His Embrace!

I wish for all of us to experience His Embrace, however fleeting the moment may be. I've stacked up a few fleeting moments in my life all adding up to "I'm in the right place at the right time doing the right thing."

Baruch Bashan—the blessings already are!

Chapter 48

Kenny's Run, More Passings, and the Beat Goes On

Carol, February 6, 2012

Tonight after I drove home from visiting my cousins in Victorville, there was a knock at my door. When I opened it, there stood Andree and Peter, brandishing big heartfelt smiles and their Redondo Beach Super Bowl Kenny's Run 2012 badges.

This was their third run in Kenny's honor, the first one being the day before we boarded Continental to Houston for that heart-stopping, telltale month of the melanoma march in February 2010. How dear of them to honor and pray for Kenny and me. How integral they were in his care during those nine months of trying to halt that never-to-be-forgotten relentless invasion. I speculated that Kenny must have been with them on the run. He always loved training his body through sports and watching others doing their best and perhaps outrunning their last race.

And how perfect to receive of their love in this very tender way after I had been with Annabelle, whose husband of sixty years had died on December 26 of multiple myeloma, a nearly always incurable form of cancer. My purpose in being there was to support my cousins, Anna, and her daughter Teresa in whatever way I could—listening, sharing my own experience, making suggestions, looking at pictures, and reading articles about Nicky. To everyone else he was Nick. To me, I couldn't call him anything else but Nicky, ever since as a child I wrote to him when he went off to the Korean War. "Dear Nicky, I miss you and I love you. Come home quick, okay?"

Teresa called me some days before Christmas to tell me her father ("Daddiola," she called him) was bad, not expected to last much longer. Did they want me to come out? I asked. Oh yes, please, can you? The next day I drove out to find them at the hospital with Nicky incoherent and in a lot of pain. They were about to send him home on hospice care. So we all trudged home where a hospice agency met us with a hospital bed and other such equipment.

Nicky was growing worse by the minute, writhing and moaning in pain. The hospice nurse exclaimed they were ill-equipped to manage his pain, so she recommended we put him back in the hospital. This time a different one, where he might receive better care. There they cleaned him up and administered some pain medication and kept him overnight until another hospice agency was arranged. This time, it was the Visiting Nurses Association (VNA).

This agency really knew what they were doing. By this time in my limited experience, I had now witnessed the workings of as many as four different hospice agencies, and I could tell the quality of care provided by VNA was outstanding. The managing nurse quieted Annabelle and Teresa's fears about giving medication, she assessed the situation and Nick's condition, and soon after, a crisis nurse arrived to manage Nick's pain levels, which were making him so uncomfortable. By this time he had not eaten in days and was not drinking, so we knew it wouldn't be long before he took his last breath.

I quickly understood my place in this family experience—I was to support them emotionally, to assist them physically as they requested, and to inwardly call upon the MSIA ministerial body worldwide to stand by spiritually to help anyone present to release anything no longer needed and to assist in ushering dear Nicky into whatever realm of Spirit was his next "grand adventure," as Kenny coined it.

So when Anna couldn't watch and had to retreat, I held her in my arms. When courageous Teresa had to administer medications, I stood by assuring her she was doing the right thing. When everyone else was asleep, I sat by Nicky's bed silently chanting the Ani-Hu and sending him Light and assuring him we were all there loving him and praying his journey now would be as gentle as possible.

On the morning of December 26, at about 9:30, I had just freshened his mouth when David, Teresa's son, noticed he had stopped breathing. That was it, his soul had ascended, no longer inhabiting his body. The man who was their husband, father, and grandfather and my cousin was gone from this world.

Today it's only been about six weeks since Nicky passed. Anna is still very tender and going through the gamut of feelings one experiences when a spouse passes. Each one goes through grief over the loss of a loved one, their husband, their dad, their Papa, or father-in-law in their own very personal way. And in all that I witnessed, I recalled my experiences with Kenny, grateful for his extraordinary exampleship in leaving this world with dignity, grace, great love, and peace.

I was also reminded that not all hospice agencies are alike. And it's worth shopping around while all principals are still coherent and able to assess the differences. The VNA team was competent, loving, compassionate, responsive, and seemed to love their work. We couldn't ask for more. These are the hallmarks of the kind of people I would want around me when it's my time to go.

There's much more to tell about my learnings and awarenesses between then (Kenny's passing in March 2010) and now, but that's still to come.

Chapter 49

Sacred Crossings—More on the Night Kenny Left His Body for the Last Time

Carol, February 13, 2012

In earlier chapters, I described what I dared put to paper about the night Kenny died. Today, some twenty months later, after a bit of training as a hospice volunteer and having witnessed the death of another loved one in my life, I can brave more recall, more important parts that may be valuable to you, the reader, that are certainly more available to my creative hand.

I didn't know then that I could give him some comfort by closing his eyes during those last hours of labored breathing when he couldn't communicate. I didn't realize I could continue to moisten his mouth. The hospice nurse left in kind of a hurry with no such instructions for me. I didn't know they would leave us at such an auspicious moment.

So when Kenny took his final breath, his eyes were wide open as well as his mouth. I tried to close his eyes, but they flipped back open twice, those incredible deep-blue eyes that I so often sank into for love and comfort, that I so often admired and could see into his vulnerability, his true loving and his powerful oneness with God.

While I could cover his body and arms with the sheet, I couldn't cover his face and couldn't look at him after my attempt to close his eyes—I was afraid I would imbed my memories with a picture I didn't want to see. It was too haunting to me—at that time, I'd rather have remembered his eyes when they inhabited his soul, his life here on Earth.

So his body lay there while some friends gathered with me in the room. We called the mortuary, because I thought that's what I was supposed to do. They were to come in a few hours. In the meantime, we told stories, laughed, cried, and waited. And everyone present, of course, took my lead and didn't look at Kenny's body either.

Aside from those haunting memories, I do remember something really important. Soon John-Roger had his aide, Jsu, call to ask "where's the body?" I told him which mortuary, and that was the end of the conversation.

Just a few days ago, Kevin and I were looking at photographs of Kenny as a young man, and I found myself recounting that phone call. In a burst of recognition, as Kevin held my hand and stayed with me in his empathy and love, I went from laughing at the photo of young Kenny doing some funny antic, to tears of understanding and gratitude. I realized once again how blessed we are to be under the protection of the Mystical Traveler Consciousness, that part of us that guides our way back to the Heart of God. For I knew that John-Roger's call was about checking in on Ken's body to see if his soul was on its way to the proper dimension in Spirit—to help it along if needed. So many times in years gone by, when J-R was counseling MSIA students in the presence of many of us, and the subject of a loved one having already passed over came up, I would hear J-R say, "I've got him (or her). He's okay. He's where he should be." And as I listened, I would well up with tears of gratitude, and I sensed so many others witnessing the counseling did the same. Thank God the Traveler chose us. Thank God we chose back. Thank God Kenny and I were devotees together. Thank God our loved ones, even if they are not actively studying in MSIA, just by being connected to us devotees, are protected as ones of his own.

Back to what I didn't know, but know better now: I could have closed his eyes so they would stay moist and more comfortable. And after he passed, if they were open again, I could have laid a clean cloth over them to help them stay closed. And I could have rolled a towel under his chin to help his mouth stay closed. I could have done a lot of things to honor his body, the temple of his soul, for as long as three days if I wanted to (legally). I didn't know this. I actually kept a lot of information away from myself because I didn't want to face his dying. For as long as he was alive, even as he got weaker and weaker, day by day, in my mind he was not dying. He would not be dying until he actually took his last breath. So I didn't ask, I didn't read much, and what I did read I forgot immediately. The only bit of compassionate education from the particular hospice agency we were assigned came from the doctor who one night only a few days before Kenny passed, told me I could stop counting liquids in and liquids out. That I should just focus on being with Kenny. Thankfully there was that much.

Only later, when I was with my cousins supporting them as cousin Nicky was passing, did I begin to get some education that mattered from the hospice agency assigned to them. They instructed on meds, on bathing and changing, on when it was time to say our last good-byes and so much more. Their loving, compassionate manner made all the difference. Their loving, compassionate manner gave me a measure of what was missing from the agency assigned to Kenny and me. Thankfully we had our MSIA ministers, our Circle of Light, our incredibly service-minded housemates. We were blessed beyond measure. Remember my talking about Circle of Light minister Diana? She recounted her experience with us as "standing in for God." And that's how I experienced my presence at Nicky's side.

I am blessed to be in a position to help others, having experienced the death of my husband in such a complex way.

And to have the gift of awareness that allows me to grow from the experience, to awaken the parts of me that were afraid and unwilling to see. In tenderness for the lost part of me that I am gradually finding and surrounding with love, compassion, and forgiveness.

So now in my memories, whenever I may picture those last hours of Kenny's life, I turn to remember the long moment just days before he passed, when he took my face in his hands and for a very long time, he held his gaze on my eyes in silent communion. The world stood waiting outside our little bubble— it could have waited forever as I soaked in the loving we shared. It shall always remain a Divine Soul-to-Soul moment when time stood still, when nothing else mattered, when his death was imminent but yet so far away—outside the bubble for now.

Bringing compassionate awareness to end of life issues is one of my passions now. Wish me well! And I send my love to all of you who over the months have devotedly supported my efforts to bring myself into a greater Light focus around death and to bring this subject, however raw the accounts, to the Light of Spirit.

Lastly, today I attended a volunteer meeting of Hospice Partners of Southern California. A woman named Olivia did a presentation on "Sacred Crossings." She calls herself a "Death Midwife" and helps families create a sacred experience for themselves of caring for a loved one's body after death. She is one among others who support people in exploring the subject ahead of time so families can make educated decisions about the disposition of their loved ones' remains.

———

—Valerie—

Thanks so much, Carol, for yet another beautiful and courageous piece. You are ministering powerfully by writing about this subject for us.

I identified with a lot of what you said. I used to live with an elderly lady, and eventually helped to care for her while she was dying. There is so much of what happened in the last few days of her life that I found difficult to understand and to handle, and only later when I read about the subject (particularly that great article that NDH published once by a hospice nurse) did I realize that what was happening was normal, and that there were things I could have done to make it easier both for her and for me.

I agree that we often don't want to know or to inform ourselves—we live in a society where many people have never been with someone who is dying and maybe never will, and so it is a taboo for us. I love the idea of a Death Midwife—someone who knows how to support us and our loved ones in transition.

Much love and Light to you on the path ahead, and always remembering Kenny and those beautiful blue eyes. Xxx

—Carol responded to Val—

Dear Val,

It's always so comforting to be consoled by one who really knows and understands from your own experience. I am so grateful to know you and consider you my friend. God bless you and Robert, Val. I love you both dearly.

—Carole Moskovitz—

Beloved Carol,

This is such an exquisite writing! Thank you—I so love reading your blogs and am sooooo excited to get a signed copy of your book!

—Berti Klein—

The relative I am supporting now is in the last stages of the dying process, so reading what hospice had shared with you plus your experience is very helpful! Estelle is going to Ruth's nursing home tomorrow to play the harp—I'm really looking forward to this!

Thank you for sharing the gift of you and the gift of my dear friend, Kenny!

Blessings and Loving,

Berti

—Ross Goodell—

What a journey you've had, and what a record you're leaving.

Love to you, my friend, and Ken's soul.

—Clara Jaramillo—

Thank you so very much for sharing such a sacred experience and for reminding me once again of what's really important. That's exactly part of the gift I received by having been with the two of you those nights, particularly the night Kenny passed into Spirit, which changed my life forever. Seeing the two of you in your most pure soul state "make love" by holding the Light, the unconditional loving and the caring you had for one another transformed me and expanded my view about true commitment and marriage. I want to believe I can have that in my life as well.

I love and celebrate you and Kenny (wherever his soul is now).

Ongoing blessings of peace, health, and love.

When we have grief, it is because we are missing someone that we valued so much in this world. Maybe they died, or maybe they have a disease that they may die from. Maybe they are going away with somebody else or moving to another country.

In these circumstances, grief is often something that says, "I cared too much." Often when we care more for a person than they care about us, an imbalance is created that can lead to grief. When you've lost somebody who has been really close to you, and you have invested a great deal of yourself in them, the depth of your grief cannot be told to somebody who has not had the experience. The feeling goes so deep it can go into the very cells of your body.

—John-Roger with Paul Kaye, *Living the Spiritual Principles of Health and Well-Being*

Chapter 50

Poem on the Nature of Loving down Here and up There

Carol, March 24, 2012

In my Consciousness, Health, and Healing class, we were instructed to choose a subject and list all the positive thoughts we had about it on the left side of a sheet of paper. On the right, we listed all the negative thoughts. Then we called ourselves forward into the Light of Spirit and began writing a poem. Much to my great surprise, since I never considered myself a poet, this was the result.

I asked for the Angel, Cherish at my back.
To help redirect me when I start to look behind me
When I see no other option but to withhold my loving
When I cannot even feel any loving.
Cherish stands tall pointing forward
Where there are no locked in memories
Where there is only forgiveness and forgetting
Where I know I am Divine.
When I cannot see you for all the shadows of myself
I put between us
Cherish points up where we are united in the oneness
Where the Light is so bright, there are no shadows.
Down here in the magnetism of the reflected world,

I know not of High Forms or God's Heart.
I am merely surviving the self-made war between the you
that is in me and the me that succumbed to despising us.
Here is where Cherish reigns, my Angel at the Gate
His arms envelop me in all surrounding embrace
Where indeed my High Form and your
High Form come into view
And together we all three travel into the Heart of God.
Such is the truth
Of why we are separate here and together there.
My darling Angel would say,
"Bring down from heaven that which
can be manifest in this world."
And Peace and Love and Forgiveness
and Tenderness and Healing
And all the Good things of the Soul shall prevail on Earth.
Baruch Bashan—The Blessings Already Are.

Chapter 51

Standing in for God

Carol, March 24, 2012

For the last several weeks, as I began to realize I was nearing the concluding chapters of this book, I ran into what would normally be called "writer's block." I thought about what I would write, I consulted my therapist on what I could write, I gathered comments from readers, and I worked on it in my University of Santa Monica Consciousness, Health, and Healing class. I certainly had gathered enough material. But, alas, I continued to tinker around with—well, it was important content, but still it wasn't the ending.

After weeks of pondering, feeling guilty, and looking at the calendar seeing that time was running out on my self-imposed June 1 draft submission date, today it dawned on me that there might be something that needed to be cleared or discovered before I could launch into finishing this wildly revealing account of a life, of our life.

Okay, a little history. In my last therapy session, even though together we have moved mountains (or healed nerve pathways, at least), we still hadn't touched upon what I experienced as blocks in my pelvic area. I was still devoid of sensation from the heart chakra down when my therapist would ask where in my body I felt such-and-such. So she suggested this week I might put my hands on my belly, imagining it was Kenny with his powerful healing touch, much as in life when he put his hand on my chest or held me in silent embrace.

Today I opened the journal where I write to Kenny and he writes back through my hand. I asked, "Kenny, can you help me get started writing about myself to conclude the book?"

He said, "Remember my hand on your chest! Do it now, my sweetie."

Dutifully I did what he said. I put both my chilled hands on my belly and waited until they warmed up. Then I put one hand on my chest with the other still on my belly. I heard Kenny say, "Now I *am* standing in for God."

I burst into sobs of gratitude for the synergy, for the all-encompassing love, for the listening and the sharing. For experiencing myself as connected through all the realms of Light right up into the God Source, through my darling Spirit of Kenny. How I am discovering, with my own eyes, myself as a Divine Being having a human experience. All this through his healing hands.

As I was thanking Kenny for this deep connection, I again heard him say (and the hearing is really intuiting through writing), "Carol, dear, my heroine there on Earth, sometimes thick and hard to reach, but when I finally get through you always open your heart to me in the most innocent ways. Have I told you lately your tears are so endearing to me? Come, my sweetie, rest in my arms where we are one with God the Comforter." And in that I began to write this chapter.

I had dinner with my dear friend Georgea this week, and I recounted the phrase "standing in for God." I first heard it coined by Diana Heil, MSIA minister and Circle of Light visitor, during Kenny's last days. Georgea suggested what a wonderful title it would make for a book or a chapter in this book. I thought, yes, but I'd already written about it at least a couple of times. Little did I know it would blossom into this chapter, while Kenny stands in for God 24/7 now, probably not just for me but for whomever he has agreed to watch over. His family, his friends who resonated with his passions, the flora and fauna here at MSIA headquarters, and wherever he is assigned.

How does this chapter draw me closer to finishing the book? How about being my own awestruck witness to the myriad ways grief immerges and submerges? Let's go there for a moment. Grief struck early, before the diagnosis, when Kenny uttered that telling phrase, "Maybe I should just kill myself."

Then as his illness progressed, it permeated every day, underneath the daily activity of his treatment regimen. Underneath my unwillingness to face what he knew way before I knew.

Then finally "agreeing" by default that hospice was the best choice.

Through those first months when I felt like I would never fill the hole left by Kenny's passing from this world.

Through many months of moving in and out, up and down, sadness, gratitude, and feelings of joy as I anticipate the future, and especially as I review the opportunities for growth and upliftment that I have been given through who we both are in Spirit—magnificent Divine Beings having agreed to love each other throughout eternity. Having loosened the shackles of karma, the purity of Divine Love with absolutely no karmic ties left in the hard realms of the physical, emotional, or mental, is at hand. What reigns supreme is gratitude and wonder, love and acceptance. And with all that comes a deeper understanding of my own process of awakening than I've ever experienced before.

I am blessed. I am loved. I experience peace in the stillness.

—Heather—

Thank you for this wonderful sharing. My own husband is very ill, and the illness has transformed our marriage and I am so committed to holding the Light with him and for him, and know that I will be with him too when he comes to his transition time. God bless you over and over sweet sister in Light and love.

Wonderful journal, Carol. I am reading more now. I feel Ken's presence too. God bless you. You are an inspiration as always. I appreciate so much what you are doing here. You help me carry on. I feel alone, and you have gone before.

Love and Light,
Heather in Toronto

—Joanne—

Loving your sharing and the ways you are continuing to learn thru observation. I've written memoir pieces about the funerals and burials of both my dad and my mom. So we are both using these powerful events for our upliftment and growth! Blessings to you,

Joanne

—Ilenya Marrin—

Dear Carol,

Thanks so much for posting these reflections on your journey. I recall early days of MSS and DSS classes, sharing lunches with the two of you, both vibrantly and fairly newly in love. I so appreciate your compassion for yourself and your process. There are a few dear ones in my life who are getting more fragile and vulnerable, dealing with health conditions that could shift into end-of-life stages very easily, and I am grateful to read of your gentle learning and growth as you supported Kenny and your cousin's family.

Much loving and Light to you and to Kenny's soul.

We can assist a person out of their grief by curing them with joy.

Joy isn't something where you say, "Okay, let's have joy," although that can work. It's more about accessing enough joy inside so that it starts trickling out. Joy bubbles up and can make the body move and transform, and that's extremely important. Some people can't handle joy. It's too electrifying and can keep them awake. It's like a sugar rush.

You may miss someone who has departed, but you also have the joy that you knew them and were able to spend time with them. I have great joy for what my parents taught me and that they were my parents. I miss them but have no grief, because they taught me what they knew. I would have grief if I didn't use what they gave to me, but I use it.

—John-Roger with Paul Kaye, *Living the Spiritual Principles of Health and Well-Being*

Chapter 52

It's Been Two Years since Kenny Passed into Spirit

Carol, June 6, 2012

I wrote to his sisters on the exact second anniversary and recounted some more of Kenny's antics trying to get my attention. Moving the little clay ducks around, souvenirs from the family's beloved Island House. Showing up on my screensaver just about every time I walked into the office after being away from my desk, either playing on the Jersey shore with his nephews or looking down at his "funny" feet. He loved to take pictures of his own feet; whether they were in those attention-getting five-finger shoes or bare, they fascinated him. And as if that weren't enough, that day I walked into my bedroom where the computer was on, and he was smiling and waving at me. Mind you, there are hundreds of photos on this screensaver.

They wrote back with their own family stories that made them smile. To this day they are great storytellers and beloved by friends and extended family. Being an only child myself and missing my extended family, most of whom had long gone, when I was with them I was warmed to be included in the fun and hilarity.

There were five kids. And there was always a lot of fun and pranks and just spontaneous occurrences that made everyone howl. I recall two that they told me about Kenny; the birthday when his grandma had baked his favorite coconut cake, and when he blew out the candles, coconut was jettisoned all over the table. And the time as a little boy, he swiped some powdered sugar donuts off the bread truck, ran under the house to eat them, and when the bread man saw the donuts missing, he and their mom gathered all the kids and asked everyone present if any of them had taken the donuts. Of course Kenny said no, but the entire front of his shirt was covered in powdered sugar. He had to fess up and never really lived it down—the subject of many family storytelling sessions over the years!

I'm beginning to experience joy. Looking back at a life full of achievement and creativity, I engaged in activities that would bring a person joy and I created things that would bring a person joy. But the nerve pathways to actually allow the experience of those things as joy were not entirely available. Therefore I misinterpreted those experiences as something like "work" or "satisfaction," but certainly nothing like joy. And set in my expression was a deep sadness evident in my eyes and even if one doesn't "see" auras, one would sense the eons of grief surrounding my countenance over incomplete relationships and unfulfilled experiences.

Always open to learning, always looking for the next awareness, always seeking to meld with the Creator, even when the pathways were clogged, this consciousness, this daughter of the Divine is beginning to experience joy. It's not like joy wasn't always present. It's that I was not interpreting my experiences as joyful. Thank God for how the Spirit has always been ready to receive me. Thank God for the thousands of ways John-Roger has made the teachings available to us. If I couldn't get it through a seminar, maybe I'd get it in a Discourse. If not there, one of his books, and if not that, a powerfully obvious experience that hurtled me into the next level of awareness under the protection and guidance of the consciousness that ushers us into the Heart of God. Insight Seminars, University of Santa Monica's master's program in spiritual psychology, Peace

Theological Seminary's spiritual science program. Initiations, aura balances, innerphasings, thirty years of working on the staff of the seminary. Through the body of work that one man propelled into being during my lifetime such that a community of thousands of students said yes, we want to support your ministry, J-R, and we will carry out the work to the best of our abilities, I am who I am today—loving myself with the deepest compassion and caring I have ever known.

The teachings of the Spiritual Heart are always available. And the learnings go on until the day we die and beyond. My life has been rich with "lifesavers" in that when I could only learn the hard way, my consciousness endured and won out and continues to win. J-R has often said, look for the pony in the pile of poop. It's got to be in there somewhere. In other words, every challenge offers a learning opportunity.

Today I heard myself saying I've lived a blessed life full of service and learning. Not that I was always learning, there were many and long, tedious intervals of stubbornness, inability to perceive the good, nagging judgments, and an oh-so-serious outlook on just about everything. But today the next thing I uttered was, "Lord, I've done so much, experienced so much grace, love, acceptance, beauty, and understanding that I'm ready to go any time now. I almost believe this and as I write, it comes clearer that since Kenny's illness I've been sliding into the most uplifting era of my life, and if that means lifting off this planet, then so be it. And if it means there's more to do here, sure as my lucky stars (nah, not luck, more like blessings), I'm once again in the right place, at the right time, doing the right thing.

From Kenny

Hi, Honey,

I love you—better now than ever before. I know you're still grieving and miss my touch, especially at night—but I'm there even if you can't see me. I treasure the time I spend with you. You know I prepared my whole life to spend those years, weeks, and days with you. I'm so glad you chose to be with me.

I know it was a tough choice and it hurt my feelings when you bragged about how long it took you to say yes, but we were tied at the hip as soon as we met and I knew it even if you didn't. That first kiss at the Church House sold me even more. "In love" was not enough of a description. "Meant to be" was not enough. "Soul mate" seems to come close. Thank you for shepherding me through those months and days. I know you couldn't face my death any sooner than you did. I know you couldn't talk about it any more than you did. But darling Carol, we both did the best we could with what we had—our ministries filled in where our personalities left off, giving us the best situation we could have, even though my body could not hold out any longer than it did. And yes, I waited until you woke up and bid me goodbye, giving me permission to leave. I held out for you as long as was needed until you were ready. Thank God and my enthusiasm and persistence for giving me the strength I needed to wait for you, my beloved wife and best friend. You were more a best friend than I was until all my blocks melted away. And then I was able to match your devotion and loyalty. God bless you, my sweetie wife.

I love you,
Your husband, Kenny

Chapter 53

It's All in How You Look at It—the Blessings

Carol, June 7, 2012

I asked Kenny what to write about to begin the process of ending this book and he said, "What if you were to look back on your life and your relationship with me and my illness and my death and all the learnings you are now aware of as blessings?"

That reminds me to mention here that I am convinced blessings reverberate throughout the universe. Can you embrace that? Isn't that remarkable to contemplate? Same is true of negative thoughts. Throughout the *entire* universe! No wonder the title of one of John-Roger's award-winning books is *You Can't Afford the Luxury of a Negative Thought.*

The Blessings

As noted in the *New Day Herald* article earlier in this book, Kenny was as much looking for me as I was for him. Our friends thought we'd make a good match, and if you believe blessings ripple throughout all creation, then it must be true the entire universe was lined up to support the match. The blessing? We both were in the right place at the right time to do the right action—to find each other.

Our friendship grew rapidly from spending time chatting about our interests, which had proved to be similar in many ways (or so our minds construed them to be) to within a month holding hands after a sumptuous Thanksgiving dinner. The blessing? Time stood still that month while we meandered through tales of our lives together. While we found infinite ways to drink in each other's essence. While we filled ourselves with memories of the last encounter until we would be steeped in the next one.

And indeed as noted earlier in this book, we assisted each other in dying at least thirty-five lifetimes prior to this one and we had been together in one way or another for at least one hundred lifetimes. It was as if we had known each other since before time!

On Leap Day 1996 at Beloved Windermere Ranch, just three months after we first held hands, Kenny proposed to me. Those three months flew by dotted by a trip to my cousins' for Christmas where he met my family for the first time, and a New Year's celebration at home-sweet-home and many evenings poring over projects for which he was my volunteer at the seminary. I hadn't said yes yet. Having been married twice before and witnessing others take their vows, and the karma that went with them, it took another two months for me to finally agree. The blessing? Patience? Or is it blindly sitting on the conveyor belt of the march toward matrimony? Perhaps the blessing is the ability to see but not see. To know on one level the lessons and blessings that were to streak through the sky like Haley's Comet racing to earth once the legal deed was done, and on another level to unconsciously ignore the star shower as each day rolled by.

I think it was the latter—for we made our bed (carved out the karma), we lay in it (met the karma with the best each of us could give to it), and what was to come was a marriage of multidimensional awareness (oblivious to solutions in the physical but willing to slog through it on every other level) that got richer with each passing day.

The marriage vows were deep, the Traveler's blessing was profound, and our purpose on earth in this lifetime was being played out, unraveling a blow-by-blow battle of wits, habits, untruths, blind furies, and pull-no-punches protective maneuvers while our souls were dancing with delight that we'd found each other, that someday soon, not more than fifteen years later, it would all become crystal clear why in the first place the match was made in heaven.

Yes, we would culminate this agreement to go into the Heart of God together by completely abandoning our conditioned relationship for one of unconditional loving, gratitude, selfless service, single focused, tenderness, depth of understanding and oneness. As for my multidimensional abilities, all this wonderment was rolling by like a 16mm movie projection while my body and mind did the tasks at hand to care for Kenny, and my emotions tried to negate the depth we were experiencing on other levels—I kept busy doing tasks that would push my grief away. Amazing how this happens. It is a result of damaged nerve pathways that limit the types of responses one has toward traumatic or even just any powerful experiences.

The blessing: to at the very least, know one is experiencing multidimensional awareness. And to at most have profound gratitude to God, to the Christ, to Kenny's soul, to my strength and endurance to emerge from the most powerful era of my life to date, whole and acutely aware of the deep and no-turning-back learning, releasing, healing, and blessings that have been and continue to be bestowed upon me.

I can truly say I am more conscious of both my strengths and my weaknesses than ever before. I can say the lessons are more tender than ever before, mainly because I am spending more time in my observer consciousness, watching how I respond to situations and circumstances. And in midstream, I'm more willing to try on new behaviors that I could not even imagine myself doing before.

Most profound is my willingness to come into the loving, even when there may be friction, maybe an insult here and there, maybe a jealousy coming my way or projecting out from me. In the last year I have consciously brought the loving to some challenging relationships in my life. And that loving has changed these relationships dramatically. With one of them, I no longer see the other person as trying to control me. With another, I forgive their lashing out at me for unexplainable reasons. Yet another was transformed by consciously coming into the loving whenever I felt left out or jealous. Compassion works wonders also. It's really a special kind of loving where our consciousness moves into the oneness and understands the other person's predicament or their response or their weakness. Our heart goes out (as it were and perhaps more than figuratively) and in that oneness we embrace who they really are, who we all really are: Spiritual Beings having a human experience.

I am blessed beyond words. My husband died; my life opened up in ways heretofore unimaginably positive. I experience more joy, fulfillment, and neutrality than I could have wished for before his illness and transition. Our nine months of complete and utter devotion to his living as long as he possibly could, my complete and utter surrender to my role in his life, and the prayer that emanated from our depths paved the way for miracles of awareness and enlightenment and prepared me for the greatest awakening of my life.

Kenny even found his way into my father's consciousness. In messages since his passing, he told me my relationship with my father was getting closer. That my dad was nearby working with me like Kenny was working with me. This opened a huge space in my heart for the loving compassion that my father deserved. Having seen mortal combat in World War II, he came back a broken man. Now they would call it post traumatic stress disorder. Then their only tool was pity. Much like my nerve pathways were blocked, I imagine his were also. So demonstrating affection toward his daughter was probably out of the question. All these decades since he died, in my own way I have abandoned my father, much like I thought he had abandoned me when he went off to war and came back two years later unrecognizable to my two-year-old self.

These realizations are blessed with healing and upliftment. I think of my father today, and instead of stoic resignation of my loss, I extend affection and love and softness with an embrace of acceptance and tenderness. And I feel that coming from him wherever he is today. Here's a piece from Kenny's messages that reflects this part of my story:

Kenny, can you help me contact Daddy tonight?

> Sweetie Carol, he's right here blowing you kisses on your birthday. He wants you to know you can contact him directly whenever you want to and he's loving you and the work you did this weekend. He will care for your little one inside. He will show you how to love her and dissolve all the misunderstandings about your body. He will bring you healing in your dreams and open up a new way of loving yourself like never before in this lifetime. He says you are loved because you are divine and oh so precious to him. You are our sweetie, baby! Together, along with your angel, Cherish, we will fill you with the loving energy of your father here and in heaven such that you are so very fulfilled. God bless you, we love you, peace be still.

The blessing: I'm still here to record these miracles. I'm still here to experience more joy and more fulfillment, and even more happiness as I move forward in my life. I'm still here to keep activating my ministry every day, keep realizing more and more of its power. And when it's my time to leave this planet for the last time, may there be a smile on my face, Light in my eyes, and a prayer in my heart to reach up into my High Form and meet those angels Kenny told me about, who will gladly welcome my soul into the Heart of God.

Chapter 54

The Last Leaving—Oneness Isn't Just a Theory

Carol, June 7, 2012

There's a magical quality about the Teachings of the Spiritual Heart. It's about the perfection of timing, Spirit's timing. John-Roger has told us that we're never given anything by Spirit that we cannot handle. So while *all* the teachings are present in every moment of our existence, the learnings are revealed to us only as we can open our consciousness to use them for our upliftment, learning and growth. In my case, after thirty-seven years of study, I am still learning and Spirit is still revealing, and if I'm lucky (stay connected) and I stay awake until I pass from this world, I will be learning right up until my last breath and beyond. And I thank my lucky stars (or should I say my good karma) that Kenny showed me the way to look forward to my own transition with joy and anticipation of the bliss that awaits me on the other side.

In all the years I have studied the teachings (more than half my life), the lessons repeat, and not only have I seen them coming again and again, they also can sting a lot harder each time until it's powerfully obvious that they can no longer be denied.

It follows then that our dying is perfectly orchestrated according to the life we have led and the teachings we have learned. Know this though, we have until that last breath to make up for eons of sleepy lifetimes and unconscious choices. I saw this when Kenny got sick. Both our lives made a bee line toward God like we've never experienced in this life. We had nine months to clean up our acts. For me that meant dropping *all* my judgments about how he led his life and coming into full and unconditional cooperation with the support he needed from me. For him, I saw him come into acceptance of his condition and alignment with his purpose of healing himself on every level possible and announce his mission to touch as many people's lives as possible with his message of joy and fun. Day after day, week and month, we rushed up the levels of consciousness such that we were listening for Spirit's direction, following it and reveling in the discoveries that only supreme sacrifice affords on a daily if not hourly basis.

John-Roger has told us in more than many seminars over the years how important it is to meditate and pray, and the more we dwell upon God and his love, when we finally reach those last moments before we leave for the last time, our thoughts will be on God, and that's where we will go, into the Heart of God. J-R encourages us to keep the mind, body and emotions clean. To do everything we can to live as long and healthy as we can to complete our karma so the record will be dissolved and we'll go free. Where we place our consciousness there we go.

And while we are on the subject of the orchestra of angels who will be waiting for us when we leave for the last time, I'm convinced that Oneness isn't just a theory. I still have trouble with time (the reality that everything's happening right now), but I'm excited to say I have personally experienced the oneness. If I leave this world with just a glimpse of timelessness, I will be most gratified and at greater peace. But oneness is evident to me right now. I experienced it (and still do) with Kenny when we were of one mind and heart taking care of him. And I experience the oneness when I'm with someone who asked me to just listen. I experience it when I consciously activate my ministry, embracing whoever and whatever is in front of me. I heard it said in my

University of Santa Monica program in Consciousness, Health, and Healing, that when we utter a blessing toward another being or thing, the blessing reverberates throughout the universe as positive energy—energy that heals, energy that loves, energy that carries compassion and understanding. How remarkable is that! Thus is explained in the power of prayer. And so it follows that when we utter a negative thought, the same is true.

In John-Roger's book, *You Can't Afford the Luxury of a Negative Thought,* one of the spiritual laws he talks about is that it takes twenty-five positive actions to balance one negative action. Better get crackin' doing and thinking good things before it's too late to catch up!

So everything we do, think, feel, and speak effects every other thing. Kind of like Uri Geller bending spoons with the power of his mind. Kind of like when we intuit a next step and it proves to be the perfect next step. Or a medium who contacts the souls of the dead tells you something only you and your loved one could have known. Or how group peace walks actually do make a difference. And talking to plants, telling them we love them, can measurably affect their well-being. How praying for one soul sends a vibration of love to all souls. How praying for the soul of a person who has left this world can support their upliftment. In my own way, in my own timing, I know I will embrace more and more of Spirit's understanding. The understanding that surpasses the mind and envelopes all space and time. One thing I know now is my gratitude is bigger than I can imagine.

The Soul is that essence of us that is a pure extension of God. The mind, emotions, and body are elements that the Soul has taken to itself in order to experience those levels of existence.

In the course of our journey on earth, it is possible to learn not to be held in bondage—or restricted by—the body, mind, or emotions. And when those lower levels are transcended, that which is left is pure Soul. Eventually, as the journey back to God continues, Soul will also be transcended, and there will be only God.

And after all has been said and done, you'll find out that you've been walking with your own Beloved for many, many eons. And one of your great realizations will be that at all times, everything was absolutely perfect within you.

—John-Roger, Loving Each Day Daily Quote, *originally from Q & A Journal from the Heart*

Chapter 55

Awake unto Love

Carol, August 29, 2012

Throughout these twenty-nine months since Kenny passed, I have mulled over the regrets I had about how stuck my mind said we were many times. Stuck in our "miasma," I called it. In my loneliness, I found myself thinking what it could have been like if we had broken out in a different way. What if we came to our senses (our hearts' desire for oneness really) sooner and we'd had more time to nurture our relationship instead of freeze in it out of fear of losing each other? What if we'd realized there was a way through our addictions that would liberate each of us and bring us closer, bring us to be allies earlier, marching toward the cause of realizing we were already one with each other. All it takes is the willingness to shift one's gaze, but only last week I learned that that shift can take eons to materialize.

I was deep in one of the last processes in the Consciousness, Health, and Healing intensive five-day lab last week—it was focused on awakening unto love. Even though the focus was to move upward in the consciousness—to come to a place of unconditional love, I was almost pressed to express these regrets. Then remembering that kneeling in prayer can activate healing, letting go, and humility, I got down on my knees and forgave myself out loud for the judgments I had been placing on myself and Kenny by regretting our "stuckness." Somehow the kneeling really moved me and what I sensed, after sensing the same awareness many times before but not as deeply or profoundly as on this day, was that Kenny's and my karma together was complete. I must have heard this from every cell of my body and throughout all systems on all levels because I began to sob in recognition that the pattern was dissolved. I had the uncanny sense that Kenny was right there kneeling with me—there was such a fullness in my heart. It was a complex experience of recognition, sadness, relief, joy, and profound gratitude.

The message went on to say that any carrying forward of our relationship is by choice and not driven by past actions. That we are to be of service together through the book and any other way it shows up to help mankind become more aware of the joys and excitement and peace in the dying process. Along with the natural human expression of loss and all the raw and normal emotions I have shared with you. That our karmic path together went back many lifetimes (those thirty-five in fact when we had assisted each other in dying and maybe the hundred more in which we'd played some significant role in each other's lives), and that's why it took such a dramatic event for us to unlock the pattern and end it once and for all. Of all the ways Kenny could have taken leave of this world or of just me, the way he did it was perfect according to the karma we'd been playing out. How awesome, my newfound freedom in the gift Kenny gave me of his leaving,

To look at the leaving from the highest perspective I can, it was perfectly orchestrated to move us into oneness instantaneously, to help me shift my consciousness from "What about me?" to "What can I do to assist you, my beloved?" And since we both were doing the best we could at any given moment in our life together here on Earth, a surprise ending that wasn't such a surprise was perfect. We had time to begin to live our relationship as we had always hoped. He had time to forgive his judgments and begin to do good things for himself, and gradually embrace his path with all his heart, mind, and soul.

But not so much time that might have threatened the deep, heart-centered, spiritual healing we both were experiencing. There was no time for negativity, no time for worrying, no time for irritation or short tempers; only actions in service, words of praise, encouragement and love, moments of oneness, each one more deeply experienced than the last, and finally the moment he left, for the very first time I heard myself telling him it was actually okay to leave.

Having a loved one die is meant to be profound. It's meant to shake us up, to have us review our life and come into acceptance. Come into forgiveness. Come into compassion and empathy. Come into unconditional loving for ourselves, our loved ones, and hopefully everyone and everything else—all circumstances and situations, every thing. And every moment we come to these cornerstone realizations, we enter into the Kingdom of God. Not that it isn't always there/here, because it is. Only that we awake unto it. *Awake unto Love.*

Blessings from John Morton

Dear Lord, bring me to Your rest. I claim Your rest. I claim all that surrounds me in my life; the disturbance, the fear is cleared away in Your power and in Your glory and Your forgiveness. Your grace bestows upon me all I need at this time. I am forgiven for my shortfalls, for my distractions, for my choices that do not serve the highest good. In You I always find my rest, my safekeeping.

Your protection is absolute. There is no fear when I am with You. I am certain that in the ways You reveal, all is being done for my upliftment and for the upliftment of everyone.

I offer up my gratitude that You receive me one more time. Baruch Bashan.

—John Morton, blessing shared at a Peace Theological Seminary and College of Philosophy class: *Intention, Health, Openness, and Prosperity*

Thank you, Lord, for revealing Yourself to us one more time, so we may behold Your majesty. How easy it is to behold. We have nothing we need to do other than to let it be, to allow Your presence to be fully in our midst. And in this presence is great joy, great peace, great love. We all have the opportunity to see the greater gifts that are coming forward. Let us take a moment to behold Your richness, the treasures from the kingdom that we call heaven, to awaken to a greater understanding of these riches as they come into manifestation. We see no limit. It is Your nature to be limitless, to be free. So it is done in ways that are always serving, and we are reminded to come into our harmony. We take this blessing of harmony into all the levels of Your creation. We hear ourselves say, "I fully accept, I cooperate, and with a new understanding, I step forward to be an instrument of these blessings, these spiritual gifts."

And on this day, let our vision be full of what can become, with understanding that it is in appreciation and gratitude for what has already been done. Your love has always been with us, never lacking. So we forgive ourselves for forgetting Your always present, unconditional loving. We open ourselves up even more to Your trust in us, that we are eternally chosen. And your choice is your will, Your will of God. We give thanks that Your will is always working in perfect ways. So our patience comes forth, along with our consciousness of empathy, always done in service; whatever is needed and beyond what is needed. We are creators bringing this forward.

So we attune to the vision of replenishing this earth, restoring what is here to be renewed, to be clarified and to be cleansed. Thou art always with us. Where we are, you are dwelling. You walk with us. We are not alone, and the way is prepared.

We take a moment with our way shower John-Roger to see his presence in our midst to see how this is being done in Spirit and on all the levels the Traveler is working. In this we find ourselves in the consciousness of the Traveler, beholding ourselves as beloved of God.

This is the simple message; we are all the beloved of God. And in his up-close and personal embrace, we are fully held and also released. There is rejoicing and great celebration. We see our friends in Spirit who have passed before us, also rejoicing in this celebration. All along the way the Beloved of God are lit up, singing the sounds of the Soul. We are home. Baruch Bashan.

—John Morton, blessing shared at a Peace Theological Seminary and College of Philosophy class: *Intention, Health, Openness, and Prosperity*

Glossary

*The following definitions marked with an asterisk were taken from John-Roger's glossary in *Fulfilling the Spiritual Promise*, Volume 3, 1291–1303. Used with permission from MSIA.

*Ani-Hu. A chant used in MSIA. *Hu* is Sanskrit and is an ancient name for God, and *Ani* adds the quality of empathy.

*Ascended masters. Nonphysical beings of high spiritual development who are part of the spiritual hierarchy. May work out of any realm above the physical realm.

*Basic Self. Has responsibility for bodily functions, maintains habits and the psychic centers of the physical body. Also known as the lower self. Handles prayers from the physical to the high self. See also conscious self and high self.

Circle of Light. The Circle of Light Program [provided by the Heartfelt Foundation] is prepared for MSIA members who enter into the process of transition. Its purpose is to have Light held in person, for the Soul, around the clock during the final days of their process—so that no one will be alone or without that Gift of Light unless it's their path. From *The Circle of Light* Handbook

Conscious dying. Rather than dropping into natural or assisted unconsciousness or sleep, we can, through Grace, stay awake, aware, conscious, during the process of transition. We can consciously participate in our process of disengaging from the physical body and our ascension with the Traveler into God's Heart. This is our Spiritual Promise from the Traveler. This is what initiates have been preparing for every time they have done spiritual exercises. From *The Circle of Light* Handbook

*Conscious Self. The self that makes conscious choices. It is the "captain of the ship" in that it can override both the basic self and the high self. The self that comes in as a *tabula rasa*. See also basic self and high self.

*High Self. The self that functions as one's spiritual guardian, directing the conscious self towards those experiences that are for one's greatest spiritual progression. Has knowledge of the destiny pattern agreed upon before embodiment. See also basic self, conscious self, and Karmic Board.

*Initiation. In MSIA, the process of being connected to the Sound Current of God.

*Initiation tone. In MSIA, spiritually charged words given to an initiate in a Sound Current initiation. The name of the Lord of the realm into which the person is being initiated.

*Karma. The law of cause and effect: as you sow, so shall you reap. The responsibility of each person for his or her actions. The law that directs and sometimes dominates a being's physical existence.

*Karmic Board. A group of nonphysical spiritual masters who meet with a being before embodiment to assist in the planning of that being's spiritual journey on Earth. The Mystical Traveler has a function in this group.

Miasma. Webster's Dictionary: an oppressive or unpleasant atmosphere that surrounds or emanates from something.

Ministry. MSIA ministers are ordained with an individual ministerial blessing that offers spiritual direction for service in the world.

MSIA Ministerial Body. A term used when referring to all active MSIA ministers worldwide. Used when referring to the powerful spiritual energy present with the MSIA ministry.

*MSIA Soul Awareness Discourses. Booklets that students in MSIA read monthly as their spiritual study, for individual private and personal use only They are an important part of the Traveler's teachings on the physical level.

*Mystical Traveler Consciousness. An energy from the highest source of Light and Sound whose spiritual directive on Earth is awakening people to the awareness of the Soul. This consciousness always exists on the planet through a physical form.

*Negative Power (Kal Power). The power of the Lord of all the negative realms. Has authority over the physical realm. Functions out of the causal realm.

*Soul Transcendence. The process of moving the consciousness beyond the psychic, material realms and into the Soul realm and beyond.

*Sound Current. Also known as the audible Light Stream of God, the audible energy that flows from God through all realms. The spiritual energy on which a person returns to the heart of God.

*Spiritual Exercises (*s.e.*'s). Chanting the Hu, the Ani-Hu, or one's initiation tone. An active technique of bypassing the mind and emotions by using a spiritual tone to connect to the Sound Current. Assists a person in breaking through the illusions of the lower levels and eventually moving into Soul Consciousness. See also initiation tone.

Resources for Further Study

Death midwifery. A service provided by companies offering education and guidance to families wishing to create green, cost-effective, and meaningful funerals at home.

Dr. Edward Wagner. Wagner Chiropractic.www.timeforhealth.com

Everyday Prayers into the Kingdom by Michael K.Thompson

Fulfilling Your Spiritual Promise by John-Roger, Chapter 14: Death

Gerson Therapy. A natural treatment that can activate the body's ability to heal itself through an organic, vegetarian diet, raw juices, coffee enemas, and natural supplements.

Grandfather. Stalking Wolf (known to Tom Brown as *Grandfather*) was raised free of the reservations in the mountains of northern Mexico. Born in the 1870's during a time of great warfare and violence, he was part of a band of Lipan Apache that never surrendered. He was taught the traditional ways of his people and excelled as a healer and a scout. When he was twenty, a vision sent him away from his people, and for the next sixty-three years he wandered the Americas seeking teachers, and learning the old ways of many native peoples. Stalking Wolf traveled the height and breadth of the Americas, living on his own as a free man. He never held a job, drove a car, paid taxes, or participated in modern society. When he was eighty-three, he encountered a small boy gathering fossils in a stream bed. He recognized that boy as the person he would spend his final years with, teaching him all he knew. That boy was Tom Brown Jr. From: www.cotef.org/about-us/about-grandfather. See also Tom Brown.

Michael Hayes. Spiritual counseling. www.awaketolove.com

Heartfelt Foundation. Founded in 1979 by John-Roger, a volunteer-driven division within the Church of the Movement of Spiritual Inner Awareness. Heartfelt is dedicated to serving and assisting people in any form of need. The Heartfelt Foundation's work and service has extended to those in need around the world. Hospitals, orphanages, schools, families and children have been visited, touched and assisted by Heartfelt in hundreds of global communities.

HeartReach. A service provided by the Heartfelt Foundation that assists those studying in MSIA who are in critical personal situations. www.heartfelt.org.

John-Roger, DSS. Founder and spiritual advisor of MSIA, the Church of the Movement of Spiritual Inner Awareness. More information at www.msia.org.

John Morton, DSS. Spiritual director of MSIA. More information at www.msia.org.

Insight Seminars. Provides personal growth seminars. Their purpose is to inspire people everywhere to a life of personal responsibility built on self awareness, loving, caring, compassion, and service. Their mission is to transform ourselves into loving so that the greater transformation of the planet into loving will take place. Their vision: a world where individuals, families, communities, and businesses work together in loving cooperation for the highest good of all concerned. www.insightseminars.org.

Loving Each Day. A daily e-mail subscription from MSIA that quotes John-Roger's and John Morton's work. www.msia. org.

MSIA. The Church of the Movement of Spiritual Inner Awareness. An organization whose major focus is to bring people into an awareness of Soul Transcendence, not just as a concept but as a practical reality. 3500 W. Adams Blvd., Los Angeles, CA 90018, www.msia.org.

MSIA Seminar. Seminars are held in homes around the world. They are gatherings for those who want to know more about

MSIA and the Mystical Traveler, and how to know God and work with the Light as an active, alive and vital part of daily life. Using a recorded John-Roger or John Morton seminar as a focus, MSIA Seminars deliver a direct and intimate experience of God and the Traveler and provide fellowship with people seeking a greater connection to Spirit. John Morton also does live seminars regularly. Schedules: www. msia.org.

MSIA Spiritual Counselings. Also known as Services. www.msia.org

    Aura Balance. A technique for clearing the aura (or energy field) that surrounds the physical body. There is a series of three aura balances, the first clearing imbalances in the physical aura, the second clearing imbalances in the emotional aura, and the third clearing imbalances in the mental/spiritual aura. Each aura balance helps strengthen the consciousness so that you can better handle everyday stress, tension, and emotional changes; aura balances also help bring the mind, body, and emotions into a greater creative flow. Because you perceive the environment through your aura, a balanced aura can give you a more accurate view of the world.

    Polarity Balance. A technique by which the energies of the body are brought into greater balance and the flow of energy within the body is enhanced. Energy blocks in the body can be created by many different things— anything from sitting improperly to thinking negatively. The effects of releasing these blocks can include more energy, lightness (as though a weight had been lifted), greater attunement to the body, and a greater ability to physically function in the world.

    Innerphasing. A technique designed to assist you in changing habit patterns that no longer work for you. An innerphasing programs out old, undesirable habits (for example, smoking, nervousness, fears) and programs in new, desirable responses (for example, greater self-confidence, more calm, remembrance of dreams). Unwanted patterns have often been conditioned into the consciousness during childhood, and they are recorded within the subconscious mind and other unconscious levels below that. An innerphasing can bring changes on these deep levels and can be an effective way to free yourself from habits that are no longer "really you" but that you can't seem to change through conscious efforts.

MSIA Soul Awareness Discourses. Booklets that students in MSIA read monthly as their spiritual study, for individual private and personal use only. They are an important part of the Traveler's teachings on the physical level.

New Day Herald and endh.org. A bi-monthly newspaper (print and online) featuring articles by John-Roger, John Morton, and other MSIAers.

Peace Awareness Labyrinth and Gardens—Headquarters of MSIA. A day retreat where people can relax in nature without leaving the city of Los Angeles. Come and walk the hand-carved stone outdoor labyrinth, find peace and quiet in the meditation garden, or chant the names of God in the Sacred Tones Workshop. Headquarters of MSIA. www.peacelabyrinth.org.

Peace Theological Seminary and College of Philosophy. Provides spiritual education to students in the Movement of Spiritual Inner Awareness (MSIA) and to the general public in order to enhance their awareness of Spirit, regardless of race, creed, color, gender, age, religion, nationality, or circumstance. www.msia.org/pts.

Somatic Therapy. Somatic psychotherapists are trained to help clients explore the bodily means by which they conduct their daily lives. Through the use of breath work; movement exercises; touch; and explorations of feeling, sensation, posture, gesture, and expression, clients experience how they shape particular identities and interact with others.

Particularly effective means of working with trauma, post-traumatic stress disorder (PTSD), dissociation, identity issues, and affect regulation. They are effective in both group and individual settings, and are especially useful as aids to self-reflection and the development of new ranges of affect, expression, and self-comportment. Taken from www.ciis.edu/Academics/Graduate_Programs/Somatic_Psychology.html.

Through Kenny's Eyes website www.throughkennyseyes.com. Contains contact information, purchase opportunities, and landscape photographs by Ken Jones

Tom Brown. American naturalist, tracker, survivalist, and author. From the age of seven, he and his childhood friend Rick were trained in tracking and wilderness survival by Rick's grandfather, Stalking Wolf (referred to in this book as Grandfather). www.wikipedia.org/wiki/Tom_Brown,_Jr. See also Grandfather.

University of Santa Monica. Founded by John-Roger, this worldwide center for the study and practice of spiritual psychology, provides innovative master's degree programs in spiritual psychology. The university's Soul-centered experiential educational paradigm evokes in students their own answers to three essential questions (Who am I? What is my purpose? How can I make a meaningful contribution?) resulting in more purposeful and fulfilling lives. Each individual student is recognized, honored, and respected for the essence of who they truly are. www.universityofsantamonica.edu.

Walking in the Light Workshop. A highly advanced Peace Theological Seminary workshop, the focus of which is imaging the Light of the Holy Spirit coursing through the physical body such that it clears, heals, and allows the human consciousness to raise awareness to the higher realms of Spirit.

Windermere Ranch. A place of peace located on 142 acres of land in the Santa Ynez mountains overlooking Santa Barbara, California. As a physical focus for the study and experience of peace, Windermere provides an environment in which one can find relaxation, sanctuary and serenity. www.iiwp.org

Acknowledgments

This book was born of "Ken's Health Blog," which Kenny began with great encouragement from our friend Esther Jantzen. The day Kenny died, I continued the blog. I kept writing because the act itself was healing, and I too was encouraged by Esther and the many friends and family who followed the blog. My thanks goes to all of them for their loving support and inspiration to keep going, exploring, revealing, and touching in to all who saw themselves in our story.

Throughout these pages, I was inspired to include the compelling and wise quotes and excerpts from the work of John-Roger, our beloved friend, spiritual teacher, and founder of our church, the Movement of Spiritual Inner Awareness. By his own admission, J-R's teachings are not new, but his knack of showing me their practical application in everyday life sustains me and lifts me daily. And his humor entertains me through tough times. I only begin to approach knowing the depth of his positive influence on my life.

John Morton, spiritual director of MSIA, touched Kenny's and my life with his deep and selfless compassion and understanding, especially during those last months while Kenny was learning about and working with his condition. John's counseling and very personal caring helped enrich our experience of the presence of God within us, something everyone can benefit from, especially at a time when so-called loss is eminent. Over and over in many different ways, he would nudge us to go with Spirit as it presented itself each day. To let go and ride the sacred wave.

My thanks to our dear friend Leigh Taylor-Young Morton, who not only visited Kenny with John in Kenny's last days but was so gracious that she agreed to lend her heartfelt voice to officiate at Kenny's Los Angeles memorial. Her love for the gift of the Apache Native Americans was equal to Kenny's and there they formed a bond of mutual admiration and respect for the life of Grandfather, a great seer in that tradition. And in her ever embracing expression of love, Leigh continues to this day to support and encourage the creation of this book.

My deepest gratitude to our end-of-life spiritual advisor, who in Kenny's last days, counseled us on what to expect, how to recognize his presence after he left the body, and to relax into the process of both of us letting go—Kenny leaving behind any obligation he might have felt toward his loved ones still here, and me letting Kenny go in his own graceful and perfect timing.

Without Saivahni, also known as Ashtar-Athena SherAn, this book may still be in its unborn state. Her encouragement through what she was foreseeing truly inspired us by fulfilling Kenny's dream of his message reaching as many people as possible.

Without my dear and generous friends, author, and inspirational speaker, Agapi Stassinopoulos, and talented editor, Anne Barthel, their encouragement, creativity, expertise, and belief in this work, I could not have brought this book to completion.

Many thanks to Greg Battes, who edited all photographs for printing, Donna Cook, who proofed every word, giving of her own compassion, loving, and professional experience, Laren Bright for his professional counsel, and Shelley Noble, consultant on both cover and interior design.

These acknowledgments must include Ross Goodell, who unfailingly led prayer communion for Ken almost daily, and our Prana family, who made Kenny's medical programs possible.

Many wonderful friends and family who were close throughout our lives and more importantly during those transformative weeks and months near Kenny's passing are named throughout the book, too many to mention here. But just know I think I can speak for Kenny when I say we are sending our love and our gratitude and the Light of the Holy Spirit to each and every one of them at this time.

Thank you to Kenny's family, who offered heartfelt support, photographs, and memories that enriched this book with real-life stories of the fun and complex family life of the Joneses.

Thank you to my brother-in-law Jim, who printed Kenny's and my blog entries as a keepsake for the family memorials that took place in June 2010. (See chapter 35, The Funeral Train Began in Springfield...) He wrote this introduction:

> *This is the internet blog that Ken Jones kept as he and his wife, Carol, dealt with the news of his cancer diagnosis, his treatment choices, and the ultimate acceptance of his impending death. I'm not sure what Ken's motivation was for starting this online diary, but it ultimately became his final ministry, and it touched many people. His willingness to share his experiences and his love was inspirational and a comfort to his family and friends. God bless you and keep you, Kenny.*

Baruch Bashan
The Blessings Already Are

About the Authors

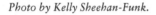
Photo by Kelly Sheehan-Funk.

Photo by Carol Jones.

As ministers and initiates in the Church of the Movement of Spiritual Inner Awareness (MSIA), Ken and Carol Jones studied for several decades the principles of living with a spiritual focus. Married in 1996 when Ken was diagnosed with melanoma cancer in 2009, their lives changed irrevocably. He began chronicling his spiritual experiences as his illness progressed and she continued writing about her experiences caring for him and the new awarenesses that flooded through her consciousness after he passed into Spirit.

Having written many courses for MSIA's seminary and facilitated them herself, Carol is now laying the groundwork for a new course focusing on "Joyful Transitions." This course will teach how to experience death as a soul journey into God's arms, exploring the perspective of the loved one who is dying and the loved ones left to grieve. Results are aimed at all involved gaining the most spiritual learning possible from the experience of losing a loved one.

Carol resides in Los Angeles at the headquarters of MSIA, where she has lived and worked on the staff of the church and seminary for thirty-two years. Ken resides in her heart.